mirai

JAPANESE COURSE BOOK

STAGE 5

SECOND EDITION

MEG EVANS

YOKO MASANO

IKUO KAWAKAMI

SETSUKO TANIGUCHI

PEARSON
Heinemann

Sydney, Melbourne, Brisbane, Perth, Adelaide
and associated companies around the world.

Pearson Heinemann

An imprint of Pearson Australia

A division of Pearson Australia Group Pty Ltd

20 Thackray Road, Port Melbourne, Victoria 3207

PO Box 460, Port Melbourne, Victoria 3207

www.pearsoned.com.au/schools

Copyright © Pearson Australia 2009

(a division of Pearson Australia Group Pty Ltd)

First published 2006

Reprinted 2006 (twice), 2008, 2009

Designed by Pier Vido

Typeset by Commercial Translation Centre

Edited by Writers Reign

Cover image by Agence France Presse

Illustrations by Christina Miesen and Moe Masano

Prepress work by The Type Factory

Set in Goudy 11.5/16.5pt

Produced by Pearson Australia

Printed in Malaysia (CTP - PA)

National Library of Australia
Cataloguing-in-Publication data

Mirai: Japanese Coursebook. Stage 5.

ISBN 978-0-7339-7066-5

1. Japanese language – Textbook for foreign speakers – English.
2. Japanese language – Problems, exercises, etc.

1. Evans, Meg, 1935-.

495.682421

Every effort has been made to trace and acknowledge copyright.
However, should any infringement have occurred, the publishers tender
their apologies and invite copyright owners to contact them.

The
publisher's
policy is to use
**paper manufactured
from sustainable forests**

Contents

Part 2　かていせいかつと おいわい　Family life and celebrations

Unit 5　日本での休み　Holidays in Japan

Unit 6 オーストラリアでの 休み Holidays in Australia

Part 3 よかとけんこう Leisure and fitness

Unit 7 しゅみ Hobbies

Unit 8　スポーツとけんこう　Sports and health

Unit 9　エンターテインメント　Entertainment

Part 4　しゃかいとかんきょうのもんだい　Social and environmental issues

Unit 10　かんきょうをまもるために　To protect the environment

Unit 11　いじめ　Bullying

Unit 12　水のせつやく　Saving water

Appendix

mirai 5

COURSE BOOK

The new edition of the Course Book:

- introduces a wide range of the most common kanji
- takes into account changes in the world and especially in technology
- has a strong range of upgraded and refined activities
- includes content that will appeal to students, including manga cartoons
- features close links between Course Book and Activity Book
- contains more higher order questions for reading passages and listening extracts
- includes a wider range of text types
- includes speaking activities.

ACTIVITY BOOK

The revised Activity Book features:

- an increased range and variety of exercises
- the inclusion of further listening activities
- a new speaking and listening activity for each unit
- increased audio material.

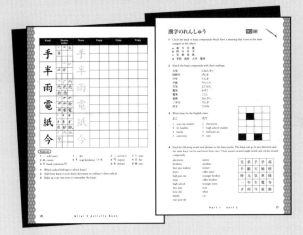

TEACHER'S RESOURCE

The revised Teacher's Resource includes:

- unit outlines to assist with work programs
- detailed notes on the suggested sequencing of materials
- photocopiable worksheets and kanji flashcards
- copies of all the listening texts
- solutions to Activity Book exercises
- extra texts related to the topics.

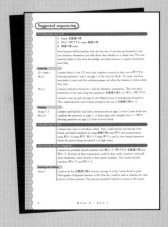

AUDIO CDS

The new edition of the Audio CD:

- features voices that are all native speakers
- contains all the listening activities from the Course Book and Activity Book
- is presented on high-quality audio CDs.

Introduction

Mirai Stage 5 is a Japanese course book for senior students. It is designed to meet, as far as possible, the requirements of the various state syllabuses. The sentence patterns, grammar and kanji introduced in *Mirai Stages 3 & 4* are repeated in this Course Book, as the amount of time provided for the teaching of Japanese in the lower grades varies among schools, and states.

Mirai Stage 5 assumes the following basic knowledge, which can be found in *Mirai Stage 1* and *Mirai Stage 2*.

Kanji

Numbers and counters	一 二 三 四 五 六 七 八 九 十 万 人 円 本
Time	月 火 水 木 金 土 日
Positions	上 下 中
Family	父 母 子 兄
Body parts	目 口
Adjectives	大 小 好
Verbs	見 行
Nature	山
Others	車

Basic particles

は　も　に　か　と　よ　の　を　ね　へ　で　が　から　まで　や

Verb forms

～ます、～です—all tenses ～ましょう
～ています、～ていません、～てください、～てもいい、～てはだめ

Adjective forms

い and な adjectives—all tenses

Counters and suffixes

～つ、～はい、～まい、～さい、～ばん、～ねんせい、～じかん、～め、～人

In this Course Book, as in the earlier *Mirai* Course Books, the furigana has been placed under the kanji instead of in the traditional place above the kanji. This is to help learners remember the kanji. If the furigana is placed above the kanji the eye tends to read it first and ignore the kanji.

In the early units, some word spaces have been inserted in sentences that are difficult to read. However, spaces between words have been progressively eliminated in this Course Book.

Finding your way around this Course Book

The following icons are used in this book.

Odaiko means 'huge drum'. It is the largest of the *nagado-taiko* (see page viii for more information about these) and is usually placed on a stand. It is played horizontally, often by two drummers wielding sticks called *bachi*. The sound is a deep, reverberating boom. The largest of the *odaiko* are found at shrines and temples; some of these weigh over three tonnes, are more than two metres across the head and cost hundreds of thousands of dollars. The *odaiko* icon will indicate your objectives for each major section and will re-sound to show you what you have accomplished by the end of each unit.

Shime-daiko. These small *taiko* will indicate the grammatical points/functions focused on in each unit.

Koto is a kind of Japanese harp. It is made of paulownia wood and has 13 strings. It is nearly two metres long and is played with three picks attached to rings on the right hand. The player kneels on a cushion behind the instrument. Movable bridges are placed along the length of each string, enabling the strings to be tuned and to resonate when plucked. It takes many years of practice to play the *koto* successfully. The *koto* icon will indicate sentence practice sections.

The **shakuhachi** is a Japanese flute. It is traditionally made from the lower part of a bamboo shoot, including part of the root. It is played like a recorder but is much more difficult. It has four holes equally placed on the front face and one thumb hole set in the rear face. Its sound is haunting and melancholy.

The **biwa** is a four-stringed Japanese lute that is plucked with a large plectrum. It is traditionally played together with the *shakuhachi*, the *koto* and the *shamisen*. In ancient times itinerant priests entertained villages with recitations of historical tales accompanied by the *biwa*.
These two icons indicate a pair work exercise, which will get you talking.

Oops! The oops icon highlights common mistakes.

This indicates a listening activity, which is on the compact discs.

CD1
track 9

Taiko

The *taiko* or drum is believed to be the most ancient of Japanese musical instruments. It is deeply connected to Japanese culture. The very size of a village is said to have been limited by the distance from the shrine or temple that the drum beat could be heard. There are two major types of drums—the *nagado-taiko* and the *shime-daiko*.

The construction of all the drums is a specialised craft but the creation of the *nagado-taiko* is particularly time-consuming. The body is traditionally carved from a single log taken from a very large and ancient tree. Such trees have become rare and very expensive these days, so some *nagado-taiko* makers are experimenting with laminated wood. The head of the drum is made of bullock hide which has been carefully prepared, stretched and attached with studs. The pitch of the drum cannot be changed after the hide has been attached.

The *shime-daiko* can also range from really large to the small hand-held *kotsuzumi*. Small *shime-daiko* are usually carved out of a single piece of wood but large ones are made from staves. Unlike the nagado-taiko the heads are lashed to steel frames and tensioned with cord. The pitch can be changed by adjusting the cord.

The *taiko* has been used for hundreds of years in Japan; its sound could once be heard reverberating across the battle fields to frighten the enemy; booming out from the temples and shrines to offer prayers for a good harvest and then, as now, beating time for the dancers at the myriad of festivals.

Taiko today

Traditionally, the *taiko* was the sole percussion instrument to accompany other traditional instruments. Today *taiko* can still be heard punctuating the drama of the *kabuki*, the *noh* and the *bunraku* or accompanying other traditional instruments at the festivals. However, in the 1950s Japanese musicians were influenced by jazz to experiment by putting together ensembles of a number of *taiko* of different sizes, thus creating a totally new percussion sound. This style of drumming, called *kumi-daiko*, has become very popular. The drum players must be very fit and disciplined and the training is similar to martial arts. The sound is exciting and the rhythms modern and creative. As a result, *kumi-daiko* clubs have sprung up not only all over Japan but in many other parts of the world, especially the USA, Canada, Hawaii and Australia.

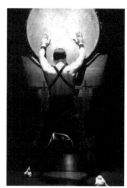

こうかん りゅうがくせい
Exchange students

part **1**

In these three units you will learn how to:
- introduce yourself
- write a profile
- describe your neighbourhood
- write letters and emails
- discuss technology
- behave in a Japanese home
- explain school rules to exchange students
- read and write a school timetable
- conduct interviews.

Contents

じこしょうかい
Introducing yourself

はじめまして

AB 3

はじめまして。山口 幸子と いいます。高校 2 年生で、16 才 です。家族は 4 人 です。父は 医者で、いつも いそがしいです。母は しゅふで、りょうりが とくいです。姉は 今年 から 大学で べんきょうしています。私は 10 月 7 日に はじめて ひこうきに のって オーストラリアへ 行きます。うれしくて たまりせん。どうぞよろしく。

AB 3

ジョン・モリスです。どうぞよろしく。高校 2 年生で、今年 16 才に なります。家族は 5 人です。弟 が 一人と 妹 が 一人います。父は 小学校の きょうしです。母は パンやで はたらいていて、おいしい ケーキを つくります。12 月 10 日に 日本に 行って、日本の 高校で べんきょうします。漢字が にがてですが、いっしょうけんめい べんきょうします。よろしくおねがいします。

Note: きょうし = せんせい
Use きょうし when talking about your family's or your own occupation.

わかりましたか

Read the introductions on page 2 and decide if the following statements are TRUE (T), FALSE (F) or NOT KNOWN (NK). Write your answers in your notebook giving reasons for any F answers and elaborating on any NK answers.

1 幸子さんは 女の子 です。
2 ジョンさんは 中学生 です。
3 ジョンさんの お母さんは そとで はたらいて いません。
4 幸子さんは 16 才 です。
5 幸子さんは りょうりが とくい です。
6 ジョンさんは おいしい ケーキが 好き です。
7 ジョンさんは 妹が います。
8 幸子さんは 大学で べんきょうして います。
9 幸子さんは ふねで オーストラリアに きます。
10 ジョンさんの お父さんは せんせい です。

1 Introducing yourself

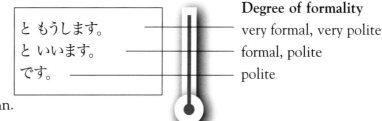

Degree of formality

はじめまして。ジョン・モリス

と もうします。	very formal, very polite
と いいます。	formal, polite
です。	polite

Pleased to meet you. I am John.

Note: もうします and いいます both mean 'call' or 'say'. もうします is a humble verb, so using it shows respect for the person or people being addressed.

わたしの なまえは ジョンです。 This is understandable but tends to be used by primary school students.

This use of 〜といいます can be written in either hiragana or kanji 〜と言います。

イディオム

1 どうぞ よろしく is an expression you use when you meet someone for the first time. It means something like 'please treat me as a friend'. よろしくおねがいします。 is a more formal version of the same idiom.

2 When you write across the page, use Arabic numbers. When you write down the page, you can use kanji numbers or Arabic numbers.

2 Expressing ability

person は   skill が

or skill は

じょうずです。	is good at, skilful
とくいです。	is good at and likes, forte, strong point
できます。	can do

1 Use とくい not じょうず when you talk about school subjects.

2 It is better not to use じょうず when you are talking about your own or a family
member's capability. It sounds as if you are boasting.

3 When complimented on your ability or looks, it sounds strange to say 'thank you'.

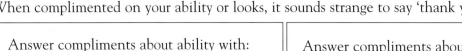

Answer compliments about ability with: いいえ まだへたです or まだまだです or そんなにじょうずじゃないです。	Answer compliments about looks with: そんなことないです。

3 Expressing inability

person は   skill が

or skill は

へた です。	is poor at, unskilful
にがて です。	is poor at and hates, weak point
できません。	cannot do

1 Ask your friends about their capabilities in various activities.

2 Working with a partner, make dialogues substituting the underlined words with words from the list below.

Mary: ケンさんは、サーフィンがじょうずですね。

Ken: いいえ、まだまだです。でも、だいすきです。マリーさんは、サーフィンが できますか。

Mary: いいえ。サーフィンは、にがてです。
でも、スケートボードはとくいですよ。
ケンさんは、スケートボードができますか。

Ken: ええ、ぼくもスケートボードはとくいです。

ピアノ	piano	スキューバダイビング	scuba diving
じょうば	horse riding	ローラーブレード	roller blades
ファミコン	computer games	サッカー	soccer

イディオム

AB 2

はじめて です。

subject	は	はじめて です。	It's the first time.
subject	は	はじめて ですか。	Is it the first time?

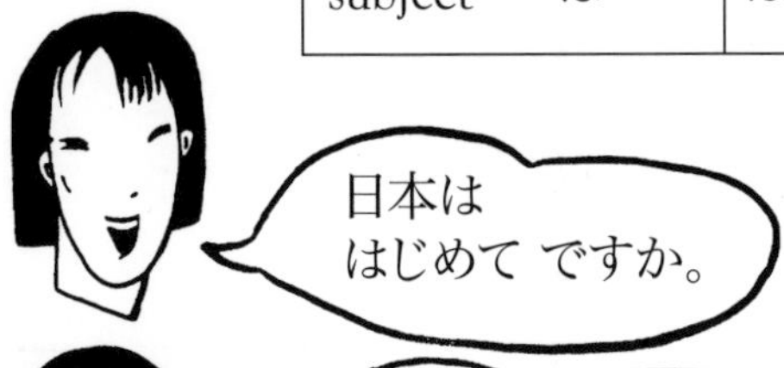

日本は はじめて ですか。

はい、はじめて です。

すしは はじめて ですか。

いいえ。オーストラリアで よくたべます。

Using はじめて to make excuses

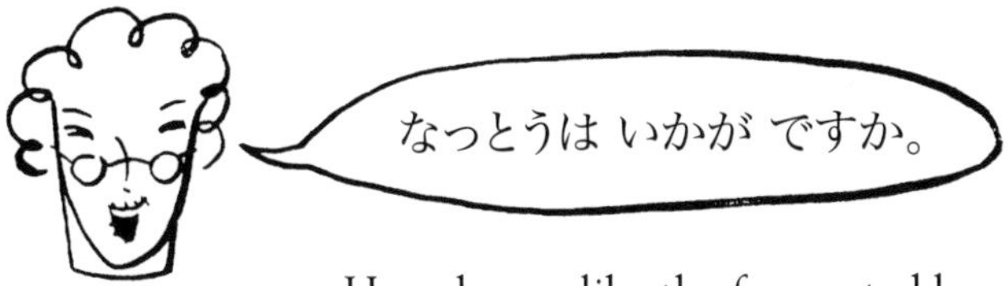

なっとうは いかが ですか。

How do you like the fermented beans?

ええと、はじめて です。ちょっと...

Well, er, it's the first time I have tried them, so ...

4 Expressing strong feelings such as joy, complaint

| て form of adjective | + たまりません (unbearably)

| (うれしい | happy) | うれしくてたまりません | I am over the moon with happiness. |
| (あつい | hot) | あつくてたまりません | It is unbearably hot. |

This pattern can also be used with the たい form of the verb.

 れい

その えいがを みたいです。	I want to see that movie.
その えいがを みたくて たまりません。	I can't wait to see that movie.
くるまを かいたいです。	I want to buy a car.
くるまを かいたくて たまりません。	I badly want to buy a car.

Express the following ideas in Japanese.
1. I am desperate for a drink of water.
2. It is unbearably cold, isn't it?
3. I cannot wait to meet Michiko.
4. Is this your first experience of a meat pie?
5. Is this your first visit to Australia?
6. I badly want to go to Japan.

Unit 1 : じこしょうかい Introducing yourself   5

5 Linking sentences to make one long sentence

AB 1, 12

To link sentences look at the ending of the first sentence.

Case 1   If the sentence ends with a verb, change it to the て form (see page 184).

あしたは はやく あしたは はやく	おきます。 おきて、	テニスの れんしゅうを します。 テニスの れんしゅうを します。

Tomorrow I will get up early and practise tennis.

みちこさんは みせへ みちこさんは みせへ	いきました。 いって、	パンを かいました。 パンを かいました。

Michiko went to the shop and bought some bread.

Case 2   If the sentence ends with an い adjective, change い into くて, drop です.

やまださんは せが やまださんは せが	たかいです。 たかくて、	バスケットボールが じょうずです。 バスケットボールが じょうずです。

Mr Yamada is tall and good at basketball.

あの みせの すしは あの みせの すしは	おいしかったです。 おいしくて、	とってもやすかったです。 とってもやすかったです。

That shop's sushi was delicious and very cheap.

Case 3   If the sentence ends with noun です / でした or な adjective です / でした change です or でした to で.

ちちは ちちは	いしゃです。 いしゃで、	いつも いそがしいです。 いつも いそがしいです。

Dad is a doctor and always busy.

ポンペイは ポンペイは	きれいでした。 きれいで、	ゆうめいな まちでした。 ゆうめいな まちでした。

Pompei was a beautiful and famous town.

Note: Do not worry about the tense of the first sentence. It will be determined by the last verb.

1 Match the most appropriate sentences from A and B and join to form one long sentence.

AB 8, 11

A	て form	B
1 デパートへ 行きました。	いって	**a** 本を かりました。
2 てがみを かきました。		**b** がっこうへ 行きます。
3 としょかんへ 行きました。		**c** ともだちに だしました。
4 ドーナツを かいました。		**d** おかあさんに あげました。
5 まいにち 3 ばんのバスにのります。		**e** セーターを かいました。
6 カードを つくりました。		**f** ともだちと いっしょにたべました。

2 Describe these illustrations using two adjectives from the following list:

- たのしい
- ちかい
- おもしろい
- べんり
- たかい
- おおきい
- ハンサム
- おいしい

ここがきよみずでらです

Listen to the conversation between Don and Kayoko.

a What are Don's impressions of the first two places?

b What does Kayoko say about the other two?

Kanji	Reading	Meaning		A way to remember
家	いえ カ	house		There are lots of people under the roof of the **house**.
族	ゾク	family		Beside the house, **a family** member is weeding. Others are shooting big 大 arrows at a target.
名	な メイ	name		At night 夕 (half moon) open your mouth 口 and say your **name**.
言	い (います) い (う) ゲン	to say		A mouth issuing words **to say**.
語	ゴ	language		Two mouths speaking a **language**. 五 tells you the reading.
高	たか (い) コウ	high, expensive		A turret **high** on a castle wall with two mouths to shoot through.
何	なん なに	what?		A person 人 opens his mouth 口 to ask **what**?
才	サイ	~ years old		Lie sticks down in tens 十 and count with your finger to find out how many **years old** someone is.
弟	おとうと ダイ	younger brother		Wind the thread through a sewing machine like the thread that joins **brothers**.

Note: In the kanji sections the most common readings have been given. The *kun-yomi* or Japanese reading is given first. The *on-yomi* or Chinese reading is written in katakana, as is the convention in Japanese dictionaries. *On-yomi* usually occur in compounds only. 'A way to remember' is just a suggestion. Try to make up your own story.

Kanji	Reading	Meaning		A way to remember
学	まな (ぶ) ガク ガッ	to learn, learning		A light shines down on a child 子 who is enlightened by **learning**.
校	コウ	school		Father figure 父, under a roof keeps order in the **school** with a wooden stick 木.
妹	いもうと マイ	younger sister		**Younger sister**'s job is to sweep round the house with a broom.
姉	あね (お)ねえ (さん) シ	older sister		**Older sister** goes to the market 市 to shop for the family.
生	う (まれます) う (まれる) セイ ショウ	to be born, life		A new peanut seedling starts shooting and is **born**.
年	とし ネン	age, year		A peanut plant at the end of the **year** has roots and is putting its seed into the earth.

Compounds

AB 7

How many meanings can you guess? Write them out in your notebook. Answers are on page 188.

お姉さん	おねえさん	高校	こうこう	高校生	こうこうせい
姉妹	しまい	中学	ちゅうがく	十才	じゅっさい
有名	ゆうめい	学校	がっこう	十六才	じゅうろくさい
名前	なまえ	小学校	しょうがっこう	兄弟	きょうだい
日本語	にほんご	大学	だいがく	先生	せんせい
英語	えいご	一年生	いちねんせい	家族	かぞく
言語	げんご	一生	いっしょう	学生	がくせい

こんにちは。じこしょうかいを
おねがいします。

私は オーストラリアのシドニー
から来ました。ミガン・ジェー
ムスといいます。十五才です。しゅ
みは、じょうばとすいえいです。

じょうばは どこでしますか。

父のぼくじょうでします。父は
うまを三とうかっていて、よく
いっしょにじょうばをします。

へぇー、いいですねぇ。日本では
どんなことをしてみたいですか。

そうですね、ふじさんにのぼり
たいです。しゃしんで見ましたけ
れど、とってもきれいですね。

そうですね。どうもありがとう。

こんにちは。お名前は。

メイリン・チェンともうします。
中国から来ました。

日本の学校は、どうですか。

勉強はむずかしいですが、とても
おもしろいです。クラブは
英語のクラブです。

ほかにどんなことが好きですか。

りょうりが好きで、うちで
時々 私のとくいりょうりを
つくります。お父さんも、お母さ
んも 大好きです。でも、日本では
にくも やさいも 高いですね。

そうですね。どうもありがとう。

わかりましたか

1 How do you say the following in Japanese?
a Please introduce yourself.
b … on my father's farm.
c My hobbies are swimming and horse riding.
d Dad has three horses.
e What kinds of things would you like to try doing in Japan?

2 Can you find these expressions?
a What other things do you like?
b Sometimes at home I make my favourite dishes.
c … both meat and vegetables are expensive.

外国人留学生に インタビュー

こんにちは。外国人留学生のみなさんをしょうかいします。一人ずつお話を聞きましょう。

お名前は。

☆ ぼくはサヤン・チタポンともうします。

お国はどちらですか。

☆ タイのバンコクです。

☆ 日本語が上手ですね。

☆ いいえ、まだ まだです。かんじが にがてです。

しゅみは何ですか。

☆ ぼくは どくしょが 好きです。それから、日本には、たくさん、ゆうえんちがありますね。ぼくは ゆうえんちも 大好きです。

日本の学校はどうですか。

☆ みんな しけんのために よく 勉強しますね。ぼくも しっかり 勉強して タイで 日本語をおしえたいです。

☆ がんばってくださいね。

わかりましたか

Can you match these expressions with the Japanese?

1 Foreign students.
2 I will introduce …
3 One by one.
4 Which country do you come from?
5 What are your hobbies?
6 There are lots of amusement parks.
7 Do your best.
8 Everyone studies hard for the exams.

6 Expressing 'try doing something' and 'do it and see what happens'

| verb て | + みます (to see) |

れい

たべて みて ください	Please try eating it.
ふじさんに のぼって みたいです。	I want to try climbing Mount Fuji.
あけて みましょう。	Let's open it and see.
スニーカーを はいて みました。	I tried on the sneakers.

Do not write this み in kanji. It is always written in hiragana.

しょうらい どんなことを してみたいですか。

Make a list of things you would like to try doing and share it with your class.

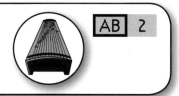

AB 2

だれがいい？

Listen to the following exchange students introducing themselves. If you could have one to stay in your family, which one would you choose? Put the students in order of your choice and give your reasons.

CD1
track 7

A やました ゆうこ

B たなか まこと

C あきもと みか

D たにぐち ゆうじ

ホストの お母さんからの E メール

	Message:			
◀ ▶ ⊡				

Subject | Profile

▼ ⊞

Sent... | KYama@nol.com

To... | Jomor@bigoz.com

▶

ジョンさん、こんにちは！
きょうは ジョンさんに ちょっと おねがいが あります。ジョンさんの
プロフィールを おくって くれませんか。かんたんな プロフィールで
いいですよ。とくいなことや、好きなスポーツなどを いれてください。
みんな とても たのしみに しています。ファックスでおねがいします！！
山本京子
P.S. プロフィールのシートが ありますから、ファックスします。その
シートに かいてください。

こうかんりゅうがくせいのプロフィール

名前: ジョン・モリス　　　　年令: 16才　　　学年: 高校 2年生
　　　　　　　　　　　　　　（ねんれい）　　　　（がくねん）

家族: 父、母、弟、妹

ペット: いぬとねこ

とくいなこと: ギター

好きなスポーツ: クリケットと テニス

好きなかもく: 日本語、すうがく、おんがく

日本でしたいこと: スキーをならいたいです。

日本にいきたいりゆう: 日本の学校に行ってたくさん友だちをつくりたいです。

わかりましたか

1　Why has Mrs Yamamoto sent this email to John?
2　Write your own personal profile in your notebook.

よしくんのてがみ

ジョンくんへ

ジョンくん、こんにちは！らい月、ジョンくんの
ところへ 行きます。ジョンくんのうちは どんな
ところに ありますか。学校から ちかいですか。
うちから学校へ バスで 行きますか。それから、
家のちかくに みせや こうえんや スポーツセンター
が ありますか。 えいがかんは？
じゃ、へんじ、まっています。
四月一日

よしより

ジョンくんのへんじ

よしくん、てがみありがとう！
ぼくは たいてい、でん車で 学校に 行きます。
20分くらいです。えきは うちからあるいて 10分
くらいです。 うちのちかくに 大きな こうえんがあって、
よく、家族みんなで バーベキューをします。それから、
えいがかんは まちの中にあって、バスで まちまで
15分くらいです。家のうしろに コンビニ があります。
えきの まえに 本やや はなやなど いろいろな みせが
ありますよ。 でも、母は ときどき、まちの デパートまで
かいものに 行きます。 スポーツセンターも まちの中に
ありますが、家のそばの こうえんで よく キャッチボールを
します。
じゃ、グッドラック!!
四月六日

ジョンより

わかりましたか

1 In your notebook draw a map based on the description of John's neighbourhood.
2 Describe your own neighbourhood.

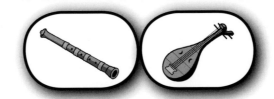

Take turns to be びわ and しゃくはち.

しゃくはち: You have applied for a scholarship to study in Japan. Give yourself a fictitious name and choose a profile from the lists below. Write your fictitious name and choices in your notebook. Give the information about your brothers and sisters using the て form as in the following example:

兄がいます。兄は 18 才で、大学 1 年生です。

びわ will interview you.

国 くに	しゅみ	とくいなこと	にがてなこと	兄弟
アメリカ	テニス	りょうり	えい語	兄 (18) 大学 1 年生
ドイツ	えいが	日本語	りょうり	姉 (20) 大学 2 年生
マレーシア	どくしょ	じょうば	サーフィン	妹 (7) 小学 3 年生
中国	じゅうどう	すいえい	すうがく	姉 (26) ぎんこうではたらいています
オーストラリア	コンピューターゲーム	ピアノ	ダンス	弟 (14) 中学 2 年生

びわ: Your job is to select suitable candidates for a scholarship to Japan. Copy the following headings into your notebook. Interview しゃくはち and make notes of the answers, in Japanese.

名前　　　　　国　　　　兄弟　　　　しゅみ　　　　とくいなこと　　　にがてなこと
　　　　　　　　　　　　きょうだい

れい

お名前は?

お国はどこですか。

兄弟は?

When you have completed your interview, introduce しゃくはち to the class.

れい

こちらは name さんです。アメリカ人です。しゅみはサッカーで、とくいなことはりょうりです。にがてなかもくはすうがくです。お兄さんがいます。お兄さんは 20 才で、大学 2 年生です。

チェックしましょう

じこしょうかい

いっしょうけんめい	with all my heart, earnestly
いそがしい	busy
うれしい	happy, glad
うれしくてたまりません	extremely happy, over the moon
きょうし	teacher
じこしょうかい	self-introduction
しゅふ	housewife
～たまりません	unbearable, cannot but – be/do
とくい [な]	strong point, favourite
にがて [な]	weak point
のります <のる>	get on, board
パンや	bakery

外国人留学生にインタビュー

がいこくじん(外国人)	foreigner
けれど	and, but, nevertheless
しけん	exam, test
しっかり	steadily, hard, firmly
しゅみ	interests, hobby
じょうば	horse riding
ために	for the sake of
ちゅうごく(中国)	China
どくしょ	reading
どちら	which
にく	meat
ひとり(一人)ずつ	one by one
ほかに	besides
ぼくじょう	farm (grazing only)
ゆうえんち	amusement park
りゅうがくせい(留学生)	student who studies abroad

ホストの お母さんからの E メール

いれます <いれる>	put in
おくります <おくる>	send
おねがい	request

ジョンさんのプロフィール

ねんれい	age
プロフィール	profile
りゆう	reason

I can:

- introduce myself formally
- understand others' introductions
- say what my strong and weak points are
- express strong feelings
- use the て form to make sentences longer
- ask if and say that it is the first time
- indicate that I don't particularly like something
- ask and say 'try doing' something
- recognise and write the following kanji

家 族 名 言 語 高 何 才
弟 学 校 妹 姉 生 年

ジョンくんの手紙
て がみ

AB 17, 25

CD1
track 9

ホストファミリーの みなさん、
こんにちは. はじめまして.
ぼくは ジョン・モリスと いいます.
高校2年生で 16才です. こんど、
ホームスティで おせわに なります. どうぞよろしく!
ところで、せいふく と テキストに ついてですが、
いろいろ おしえてくださいませんか.
それから、まいしゅう お金は どのくらい いりますか?
バスだいと 電車ちんは、うちから 学校まで いくらですか?
すみませんが いろいろ しらせてくださいませんか.
12月10日の あさ 9時半に なりたに つきます.
ごっごうは いかがでしょうか? どうぞ、しらせてください.
では、よろしく おねがいします.
みなさん、お元気で. さようなら.
　　　　10月20日

　　　　　　　　ジョンより

わかりましたか

Read the letter from John to his host family in Japan. In your notebook, indicate if the following statements are TRUE (T) or FALSE (F). For every F answer give your reasons.

1　The writer is John Forrest.

2　He is in grade 10.

3　He is writing to find out about the cost of textbooks and uniforms.

4　He wants to know how far it is from the house to school.

5　He is arriving at 9.30 on 12 October.

7 Expressing gratitude

みなさんにおせわになります。	Thank you all, for your (promised) kindness.
おせわになります。	Thank you for looking after me. (future)
おせわになりました。	Thank you for looking after me. (past)

8 Asking if it is convenient

AB 24(3)

ごつごうは いかが でしょうか Is this convenient for you?

つごう *convenience*

ご is an honorific prefix like the お in おなまえ your name.

Note: In general, お comes before words in Japanese origin, ご before words of Chinese origin.

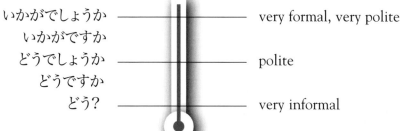

How about?

いかがでしょうか	very formal, very polite
いかがですか	
どうでしょうか	polite
どうですか	
どう?	very informal

Benri means 'convenient' as in 'handy'. It cannot be used to ask if something is convenient.

✗ あなたに べんり ですか。
✓ ごつごうは いかがですか。   Is it convenient for you?

イディオム

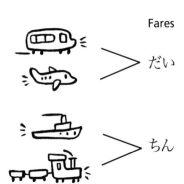

Fares

だい

ちん

Both だい and ちん mean 'cost' or 'fare' but だい is usually used for bus and air fares while ちん is usually used for sea and train fares. There is a phonetic change with ふね. It becomes ふなちん.

だい is also used for electricity costs, 電気だい, and phone costs, 電話だい.

9 Making requests

In English, when you make requests to strangers or to people you do not know well you have to speak more formally or politely than to close friends. It is the same in Japanese.

Polite approach	verb te +	one of the following	
すみませんが、	それを みせて	くださいませんか。	formal, polite
すみませんが、	それを みせて	くれませんか。	polite
ちょっと、	それを みせて	くれない?	informal

Excuse me, would you (won't you) please show me it?

Note:

1 The verb form くださいませんか is more polite than ください. The informal verb that has the same meaning is くれます. They both mean 'give me'.

2 すみません, ちょっと〜〜〜 is also often said in polite conversation.

Practise asking different people to do things for you using the pictures.

Hint: You could use the following verbs: 見せます、とります、おしえます、かします

れい

To a teacher:　　　　すみませんが、このもんだいを おしえて くださいませんか。
To an acquaintance:　ちょっと、てつだって くれませんか。
To your friend:　　　ちょっと、そのとけいを みせて くれない?

to your host brother

to your cousin

to your friend

to a policeman

* まいごに
　なりました。　* I'm lost

to a teacher

to a shop assistant (be polite)

10 Asking/telling about

noun	+ について

れい

日本について おしえて くださいませんか
Please tell me about Japan.
せいふくと テキストについて おしえて くださいませんか。
Please tell me about school uniforms and textbooks.

You are writing an essay about Japan. Ask your Japanese pen friend to tell you about the following things using 〜について.

れい

日本のりょうりについて おしえてください。

1 日本のロックグループ
2 学校のきそく
3 日本のクリスマス
4 高校生のしゅみ
5 日本のゆうえんち

Which is correct to express gratitude?

ありがとう。??
ありがとうございます。??
ありがとうございました。??

ありがとう ございます expresses thanks for
some present or future kindness.
ありがとう ございました expresses thanks for
a past kindness. Both are formal.
To close friends or family you just say ありがとう.

どうも ありがとう means 'thank you very much'.
どうも by itself can also be used for saying 'thanks'.

このあいだは どうも
ありがとうございました。

It is usual to thank
people *again* when
you meet them.

Mrs Yamamoto answers John's letter AB 17

山本さんのへんじ

ジョンさん、お手紙ありがとう。日本では 今 もみじがとてもきれいです。でも すこしさむくなりました。オーストラリアはどうですか。毎日あついですか。

さて、せいふくとテキストについてですが、ぜんぶありますから買わなくてもいいですよ。お金はあまりつかわないほうがいいですね。

バスだいと電車ちんは毎週千五百円くらいですね。でも、東京の冬はとてもさむいからオーバーをわすれないでね！

あさ、九時半はちょっと早いけど、だいじょうぶ！みんなでむかえに行きます。では、ジョンさん、成田で会いましょう！たのしみにしています。じゃ、気をつけてね。

十月二十八日

山本京子

わかりましたか

Can you find these expressions in the letter above?
1 The maple trees are very beautiful now.
2 Well now, about the uniforms and textbooks.
3 Don't forget to bring an overcoat.
4 We are looking forward to it.
5 It is better not to spend a lot of money, isn't it?
6 We will all come to meet you.
7 Because the winter in Tokyo is very cold …

In pairs, prepare the dialogue of a phone call between yourself and Mrs Yamada in which you ask questions about clothes, money, the school and the family you will stay with.

11 Giving a reason

Add から to the end of the sentence that gives the reason.

Reason	Consequence
せいふくは ありますから	かわなくてもいいです。
I have a uniform so	there is no need to buy one.
あめがふっていますから	そとへ行きたくないです。
It is raining so	I don't want to go outside.

The reason can come at the beginning of the sentence as in the above examples or at the end.

Consequence	Reason
せいふくは かわなくてもいいです。	ありますから。
You don't have to buy a uniform	because I have one.
そとへいきたくないです。	あめがふっていますから。
I don't want to go outside	because it is raining.

Be careful where you place から. For example, if you express 'I don't want to go outside because it is raining' as そとへ いきたくない から あめが ふっています。 you are saying 'It is raining because I don't want to go outside'!

---

1 Complete the following sentences, giving the reason.

れい

…から ジャケットを きてください。
きょうは ゆきが ふっていますから
ジャケットを きてください。

a …から はやく ねましょう。
b …から オーストラリアが 好きです。
c …から まいにち ピアノの れんしゅうを
　 しました。
d …から バスケットボールが とくいです。
e …から このしゅくだいを てつだって
　 くれない?

2 Complete the following sentences giving a consequence for each one.

れい

もみじがとてもきれいですから…
もみじがとてもきれいですから、ピクニック
に行きましょう。

a もうすぐ テストがありますから…
b かんじは あまりれんしゅうしません
　 でしたから…
c この かんじが わかりませんから…
d がいこくに きょうみが ありますから…
e はじめてですから…

12 Giving advice

> 1 Please don't …
> 2 You had better not …
> 3 You don't have to …
> 4 It doesn't matter if you do or not.

To make these sentences, use the plain negative or *nai* form of verbs.
How to make the plain negative? See page 183.

Advice 1 Please don't …

Verb ない	+ で ください。

（れい）

ここで たべないで ください。	Please do not eat here.
ドアを あけないで ください。	Please do not open the door.

Advice 2 You had better not …

Verb ない	+ ほうが いいです。

（れい）

おかねは あまり つかわない ほうが いいです。	You had better not use too much money.
きょうは 行かない ほうが いいです。	You had better not go today.

Advice 3 You don't have to …

Verb な~~い~~ く	+ ても いいです。 (even if you don't it is okay)

Note:
きます (wear) → きなくても いいです。
きます (come) → こなくても いいです。

（れい）

せいふくをきなくてもいいです。	You don't have to wear a uniform.
あしたこなくてもいいです。	You don't have to come tomorrow.
テキストをかわなくてもいいです。	You don't have to buy a textbook.

Advice 4 It doesn't matter if you do or not.

Verb て	+ も	verb な~~い~~ く	+ ても いいです

（れい）

たべても たべなくても いいです。	It doesn't matter if you eat it or not.

1 Complete the dialogues in the pictures below, using the following example as a guide.

れい

A: ここでおよぎましょうか。

Shall we swim here?

B: いいえ、あぶないから、およがないほうがいいです。

No, it's dangerous. We had better not.

or いいえ、ここはあぶないから、およがないでください。

No, it's dangerous. Don't swim here.

2 Substituting the words listed below, make dialogues like the following.

れい

A: ベジマイトは たべなくてもいいですか。

Is it all right if I don't eat the Vegemite?

B: いいですよ。たべなくてもいいです。たべてもたべなくてもいいです。

It is okay, you don't have to. It doesn't matter if you eat it or not.

a	さしみ	たべます	f	このえいが	見ます
b	せいふく	きます	g	日本語	かきます
c	ネクタイ	します	h	うま	のります
d	くつ	はきます	i	このおちゃ	のみます
e	6 じ	おきます	j	学校	行きます

Note: Particle は is used instead of を or が in negative sentences. は means 'as for'.

In the case of other particles there is no change, for example おはしでたべなくてもいいです。

イディオム

| むかえに 行きます/きます | coming to meet you |
| おくりに 行きます/きます | seeing someone off |

The choice of 行きます or きます depends on the movement of the speaker. If the speaker has to go somewhere to meet or see someone off, 行きます is used. This is always so, even though in English you might say 'I'll come to the airport to meet you' or 'I'll come to the airport to see you off'.

13 Looking forward to something

Thing を	たのしみに	しています。or まっています。or してまっています。

れい

| パーティーをたのしみにしています。 | I am looking forward to the party. |
| おへんじをたのしみにまっています。 | I am forward to your reply. |

おへんじをまっています

Sachiko sends three voice messages to her friends' mobile phones. Imagine that you are each of the following people. Listen to your message.

1   You are Oscar: What does she ask you to do?

2   You are Emma: What favour does she ask you? When does she want you to do it?

3   You are Janelle: What news does she give you? What does she ask you to do? What advice does she give you? What reason does she give for this advice?

Writing letters and emails to friends and acquaintances

Japanese people display their personality and warmth through their choice of expression, just like writers in any other language. When writing to someone they do not know well, they choose polite expressions and verb endings to show respect for the person they are addressing. When writing to close friends and family members, they often use a mixture of polite and familiar language. When writing your first letter to someone you should write in polite style, but as you become friends you can express your friendly feelings by choosing less formal expressions.

There is no equivalent for 'Dear …'. Just write the person's name followed by さん or ちゃん if the person is a close friend who is younger than you. For email there is no need to include the date, and the name of the writer is usually placed on the left-hand side.

Expressions used in letters

Polite style to acquaintances | | Informal style to close friends

Polite style to acquaintances	Topic	Informal style to close friends
お元気ですか。 げんき	← Asking about health →	(お)元気？ げんき
オーストラリアは 今 夏で いま なつ とてもあついです。そちら は いかがですか。 or こちらは ずいぶんさむく なって きました。そちら は もう夏ですか。	← Talking about the weather → こちら here そちら there	オーストラリアは 今 夏で いま なつ とてもあついです。そちらは どう？ こちらは ずいぶん さむく なってきましたよ。そちらは もう夏でしょうね。
では、きょうは これで しつれいします。 おからだをたいせつに。 みなさんに よろしく おつたえください。	← Closing remarks → That's all for today. Take care. Regards to all.	では、きょうはこれで。 じゃ、お元気で。 げんき みなさんによろしく。

date ⟶ | 8月1日
秋子より | ← from Akiko

漢字

かんじ

Kanji	Reading	Meaning		A way to remember
春	はる シュン	spring		三 three 人 people walking in the **spring** 日 sunshine.
夏	なつ カ	summer		A hat over the 目 eyes in **summer**.
秋	あき シュウ	autumn		After the rice is harvested the stubble is burned in **autumn**.
冬	ふゆ トウ	winter		Snow on the mountain in **winter**.
天	テン	heaven		That which is above all that is big 大, **heaven**.
気	キ	spirit, energy		Put the lid on the boiling rice to keep the **energy** from escaping.
元	もと ゲン	origin, source, foundation		The roots of a tree are its **foundation**.
時	とき ジ	time, when, o'clock		日 sun on the left, 寺 temple on the right; the temple gong told the **time**.
半	ハン	half		Each side is **half** of the other, like your face.

Kanji	Reading	Meaning		A way to remember
手	て シュ	hand		A picture of a **hand** on the cave wall.
紙	かみ シ	paper		Using 糸 threads of plants, spread on a frame to make **paper**.
雨	あめ ウ	rain		The heavens with **rain** falling, and a shelter.
電	デン	electricity		In the rain storm a flash of **lightning** hits the paddy field.
今	いま コン	now		**Now** he has a moustache above his mouth.

Compounds

AB 21–22

1 How many meanings can you guess?

天気	てんき	元気	げんき	一時	いちじ
二時半	にじはん	五時間	ごじかん	何時	なんじ
手紙	てがみ	(お)手洗い	(お)てあらい	手足	てあし
上手	じょうず	下手	へた	今年	ことし
今月	こんげつ	今週	こんしゅう	今日	きょう
電気	でんき	電話	でんわ	電車	でんしゃ

2 Can you read these names?

a 秋子   **b** 春子   **c** 秋山

d 夏目   **e** 冬川   **f** 春木

Email from Japan

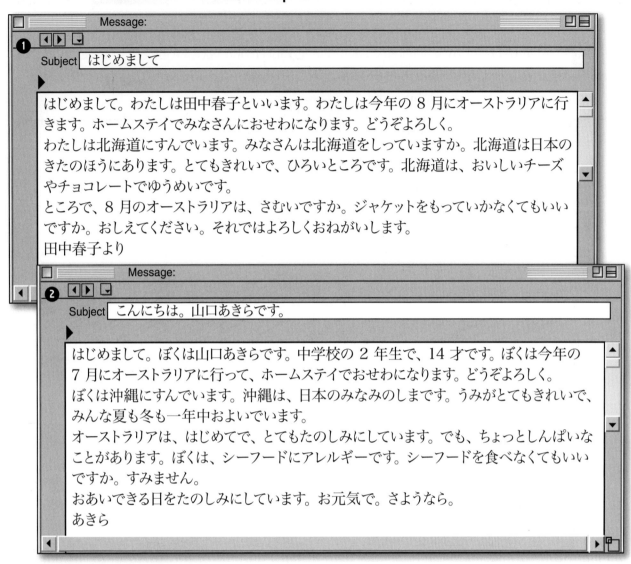

Message:

❶

Subject: はじめまして

はじめまして。わたしは田中春子といいます。わたしは今年の 8 月にオーストラリアに行きます。ホームステイでみなさんにおせわになります。どうぞよろしく。
わたしは北海道にすんでいます。みなさんは北海道をしっていますか。北海道は日本のきたのほうにあります。とてもきれいで、ひろいところです。北海道は、おいしいチーズやチョコレートでゆうめいです。
ところで、8 月のオーストラリアは、さむいですか。ジャケットをもっていかなくてもいいですか。おしえてください。それではよろしくおねがいします。
田中春子より

Message:

❷

Subject: こんにちは。山口あきらです。

はじめまして。ぼくは山口あきらです。中学校の 2 年生で、14 才です。ぼくは今年の 7 月にオーストラリアに行って、ホームステイでおせわになります。どうぞよろしく。
ぼくは沖縄にすんでいます。沖縄は、日本のみなみのしまです。うみがとてもきれいで、みんな夏も冬も一年中およいでいます。
オーストラリアは、はじめてで、とてもたのしみにしています。でも、ちょっとしんぱいなことがあります。ぼくは、シーフードにアレルギーです。シーフードを食べなくてもいいですか。すみません。
おあいできる日をたのしみにしています。お元気で。さようなら。
あきら

わかりましたか

Can you match these expressions in email 1?
a   Hokkaido is in the north of Japan.
b   It is a very beautiful and spacious place.
c   By the way,
d   Is it okay if I don't bring my jacket?
e   Thank you for the homestay.
f   Hokkaido is famous for its delicious cheese and chocolate.

Can you match these expressions in email 2?
1   Okinawa is the Southern Island.
2   All year round.
3   I am looking forward to the day we meet.
4   Is it okay if I don't eat seafood?
5   There is something I worry about.
6   I am allergic to seafood.
7   This is the first time (visiting Australia).

Imagine you are going to Japan as an exchange student. Using the emails as a model, write an email to your host family.

Communication in the past and now

John's new school in Japan has a number of exchange students. The school organises classes in Japanese at three levels for these students: beginner, advanced and very advanced. In order to know where to place John the school has asked him to write an essay in Japanese on 'Communication in the past and now'. This is what John wrote.

ぼくたちのコミュニケーション、今とむかし

今、ぼくたちは、いろいろなほうほうで、ともだちや家族とれんらくします。ぼくは、ともだちと、けいたい電話やインターネットのチャットルームをつかって、はなします。まえは、けいたい電話だいが高かったから、あまりつかいませんでした。でも、今電話だいは、やすくなりました。けいたいのメールや、E メールも、あまり高くなくて、べんりです。

　20 年ぐらいまえ、E メールやチャットルームはありませんでした。ふつうの人は、けいたいをもっていませんでした。人々は、手紙と電話をつかっていました。たとえば、オーストラリアから、日本に手紙をおくりました。そうすると、1 しゅうかんぐらいかかりました。そとから電話をかけたい時、こうしゅう電話をさがしました。とてもふべんでした。

　ぼくは今、日本からオーストラリアの家族によく E メールをおくります。学校やホストファミリーのしゃしんも、スキャンしておくります。妹や弟から、すぐにへんじが来て、うれしいです。さいきん、ぼくのそぼもコンピューターをかって、E メールをはじめました。そして、ぼくの E メールやしゃしんのスキャンをとてもたのしみにしています。

　テクノロジーがはったつして、ぼくたちのせいかつはとてもべんりになりました。テクノロジーをじょうずにつかって、たのしくコミュニケーションしたいですね。

たんご

けいたい	mobile, portable	たとえば	for example
こうしゅう	public	はったつ	progress
ぐらい	approximately	人々 (ひとびと)	people
さいきん	recently	ふべん	inconvenient
さがします	search	ほうほう	method
せいかつ	life	れんらく	contact
そうすると	and so, if you did this	電話 (でんわ)	phone

わかりましたか

Read John's essay and answer the following questions.

1 What methods does John use to keep in contact with his friends?

2 What changes have occurred in these methods?

3 How does John describe the world of 20 years ago?

4 How does John's family feel about him being in Japan?

5 What is John's opinion of technology?

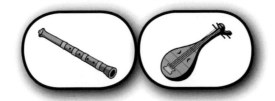

びわ: In your notebook make a list of your family members. Next to each name state the number of times a week approximately that each person uses the following communication technology. Use the following example as a guide.

	インターネット Internet	Eメール email	チャットルーム chatroom	けいたい電話 mobile phone	けいたいのメール text message
父	つかいません	つかいません	つかいません	まいにち	まいにち
母	2 回 <small>かい</small>	7 回	つかいません	つかいません	つかいません
妹	7 回	7 回	7 回	まいにち	まいにち
弟	2 回	7 回	3 回	5 回	5 回
そふ	7 回	7 回	つかいません	つかいません	つかいません

しゃくはち: You have been asked to conduct a marketing survey to find out if there is a correlation between age and the use of communication technology. Start by asking びわ how many there are in the family and their approximate ages. Write down the information in your notebook. Then ask びわ how many times a week each family member uses the following communication technology. Use the following example as a guide.

れい

しゃくはち:	家族は何人ですか。
びわ:	六人です。父と母と姉と弟とそふがいます。
しゃくはち:	お父さんは 何才ですか。
びわ:	四十六才です。
しゃくはち:	お父さんは、まいしゅう、何回インターネットをつかいますか。
びわ:	父はインターネットをつかいません。
しゃくはち:	けいたい電話をつかいますか。
びわ:	はい、まいにち、しごとでつかいます。
しゃくはち:	けいたいのメールもつかいますか。
びわ:	はい、まいにちつかいます。

Record the information in a table such as this:

家族の人 family member	年令 <small>ねんれい</small> age	インターネット Internet	Eメール email	チャットルーム chatroom	けいたい電話 mobile phone	けいたいのメール text message
お父さん	46 才	0	0	0	まいにち	まいにち

チェックしましょう

ジョンくんのてがみ

いります ＜いる＞	to need
おせわになります	thank you for your (promised) kindness
(お) 元気で げん き	'Take care'
こんど	shortly, soon
しらせます ＜しらせる＞	to let know, inform
せいふく	school uniform
つごう	convenience
ところで	by the way
～について	about …

手紙と E メール

アレルギー	allergy
いちねんじゅう (一年中)	all year
きた	north
ところ	place
しま	island
ずいぶん	extremely
そちら	there (polite)
(お) ねがい	request
ひろい	spacious
ほう	direction
みなみ	south

山本さんのへんじ

あいます ＜あう＞	to see, meet	むかえにいきます ＜行く＞ い	to go to meet/ welcome
気をつけて き	take care, be careful	もみじ	maple tree/leaves
さて	Well now		
たのしみ	enjoyment		

I can:

- make requests
- identify a topic using 'about'
- thank someone for looking after me
- ask if it is convenient
- state reasons and consequences in one sentence
- give advice
- say I will see people off or come to meet them
- say I am looking forward to something
- write a letter to a host family
- understand emails, faxes, letters and essays
- read and write the following kanji

春 夏 秋 冬 天 気 元
時 手 紙 半 雨 電 今

きそく
Rules

ジョンくんとスリッパ

John arrives at Yamamoto's home.

わかりましたか

1 Read the cartoon and, in your notebook, indicate if the following sentences are TRUE (T) or FALSE (F). Give reasons for F answers.
The characters said the following.
   a 'How do you do John. I am Grandma.'
   b 'Welcome. You must be tired.'
   c 'John, you don't have to take off your shoes here.'
   d 'How do you do. I am John.'
   e 'How small your house is.'
   f 'Shall I bring the baggage?'
   g 'Put your shoes in the getabako please.'
2 Discuss this question with your friends: Why does Obaasan say, 'Please come up'?

14 Expressing obligation

'We/I must/have to'
'You must/have to'

verb　なⅴ ければ なりません ──────── formal,
verb　　　ないと いけません ──────── polite
verb　　なⅴ くちゃ or なきゃ ──── informal

 れい

1　手紙をかかなければなりません。　　　We/I/you have to write a letter. (formal)
2　くつをぬがないといけません。　　　We/I/you have to take off our shoes. (polite)
3　べんきょうしなくちゃ。　　　　　　We/I/you have got to study. (informal)

The addition of か to sentences 1 and 2 turns them into questions.

れい

あした何時におきなければなりませんか。

What time do I/you have to get up tomorrow?

バスにのらないといけませんか。

Do I/you have to take the bus?

1　In pairs talk about your plans for tomorrow. Use the following example as a guide.

れい

A: あした、いっしょに えいがを 見に 行き
　ません か。
　Let's go to the movies tomorrow.
B: あしたは、しゅくだいを しなければなり
　ません。
　Tomorrow I have to do my homework.
A: ああ、そうですか。ざんねんですね。
　Oh really? What a shame.

a　へやのそうじをします。
b　テストのべんきょうをします。
c　パーティーのケーキをつくります。
d　くうこうに さち子さんをむかえに行きます。

2　There is to be a welcome party for exchange students at your school. Discuss with your friends what you have to do for the party using なくちゃ.

…をかいます。
…をつくります。
…をもってきます。
…をきれいにします。
デコレーションをへやに かざります。

15 Apologising

ごめん。 Sorry (to a friend)

ごめんなさい。 I'm very sorry (formal)

すみません。 Excuse me.

すみません is also used when thanking someone. Excuse me (for putting you to so much trouble).
Similar to 'You shouldn't have'.

しつれいします。 Excuse me (I am about to disturb you).

しつれいしました。 Excuse me (I disturbed you).

16 Accepting apologies

いいです。 It is all right.

だいじょうぶ。 That's okay.

しんぱいしないで下さい。 Don't worry.

しんぱいしなくてもいいです。 You don't have to worry.

17 Prohibition, denial

AB 37

You/we should not …

You/we are not allowed to …

verb	て + は いけません。

れい

うちの中で くつをはいては いけません。 Inside the house you should not wear shoes.

きょうしつで ねては いけません。 In the classroom you should not sleep.

In speech there is no break between て and は.

---

1 You are about to play basketball (or soccer) with some exchange students. Try to explain the rules in Japanese using …てはいけません…ても いいです。

サッカー

ボールをてで (もちます)

あたまを (つかいます)

ボールをあしで (けります)

ゴールキーパーはボールをてで (もちます)

バスケットボール

ボールを (もちます)

ボールをもって (はしります)

ボールを (なげます)

ドリブルを (します)

2 Try to explain the rules of other sports in Japanese.

ジョンくんとスリッパ 3

レッド ヒル高校の校則
こうそく

At Red Hill High School the sports teacher has written the school rules in Japanese for the Japanese exchange students.

レッド ヒル高校の校則
こうそく

1　8 時 30 分までに 学校に来なければ なりません。
2　たばこはぜったいに すっては いけません。
3　わるい ことばを 使っては いけません。
4　学校で チューインガムを かんでは いけません。
5　ごみは ごみばこに 入れなければ なりません。
6　つくえや かべに らくがきを しては いけません。
7　昼ご飯は きょうしつの 外で食べなければ なりません。
8　けいたい電話は きょうしつに もってきては いけません。
9　宿題は まいにち しなければ なりません。
　　しゅくだい

ふくそうについて

1　ぼうしを かぶらなければ なりません。
2　おけしょう、マニキュア、アクセサリーを しては いけません。
3　いろいろな いろの リボンや ヘヤーバンドを しては いけません。
4　ピアスは 1 くみだけつけても いいです。

わかりましたか

1　Which rules are the same as the rules in your school?
2　Which rules are the same as the rules in the Japanese school described on page 39?
3　Are there any rules that are the opposite?
4　Can you find how to say the following?
   - smoking
   - graffiti
   - rubbish
   - make-up
   - earrings.

Your school is to host a group of Japanese exchange students. Write out the school rules for them in Japanese so that they will not make any mistakes.

第一高校の校則
だいいち　　　こうそく

Here are the school rules for Daiichi Senior High School in Japan. Students have these written in their school diary, which they are supposed to have with them every day.

第一高校の校則
だいいち　　　こうそく

1　ちこくをしてはいけません。
2　バイクで学校にきてはいけません。
3　学校でチューインガムをかんではいけません。
4　たばこをすってはいけません。
5　ろうかをはしってはいけません。
6　けんかをしてはいけません。
7　アルバイトをしてはいけません。
8　けいたい電話は学校にもってきてはいけません。

ふくそうについて
1　いつもせいふくをきなければなりません。
2　おけしょう、マニキュア、ピアスをしてはいけません。
3　かみのけをそめてはいけません。
4　しろいくつ下をはかなければなりません。

わかりましたか

1　Which rules are the same as the ones in your school?
2　Which rules are different?

日本のしゅうかんときそく

Imagine that you have just arrived in Japan as an exchange student. You are taken to a reception room where you and other exchange students are given advice about how you should behave in your host families' homes and in your new schools.

Copy the following chart into your notebook and fill it in according to what you understand.

CD1
track 16

	Must not	Must	Other advice
うちで			
学校で			

さちこさんの日本の高校の時間わり
じかん

Read Sachiko's Japanese timetable and answer her questions.

これは私の高校、さくら山高校の 1 年生の時間わりです。

	月	火	水	木	金
1 8:30–9:20	英語 1	数学 すうがく	国語 1	ほけん	せかいし
2 9:30–10:20	たいいく	ぶつり	せいぶつ	りんり	英語 1
3 10:30–11:20	こてん	りんり	OCB	しょどう	数学 すうがく
4 11:30–12:20	かていか	たいいく	数学 すうがく	しょどう	たいいく
12:20–13:10	ひる休み				
5 13:10–14:00	せかいし	おんがく	こてん	数学 すうがく	国語 1
6 14:10–15:00	せいぶつ	国語 1	びじゅつ	ちり	ぶつり

このあと、学校のそうじやクラブかつどうをします。クラブはたいてい五時半まで、やっています。
みんな 6 時までにうちにかえらなければなりません。
みなさんのじかんわりと、ちがいますか。よく、にていますか。
1 年生は、12 かもくから 14 かもく、べんきょうしています。
みなさんは、何かもく、べんきょうしていますか。
高校 2 年生から、せんたくかもくがあります。私は、すうがく や りか が にがてですから、英語や
びじゅつをせんたくしたいです。
みなさんの学校では、どんなせんたくかもくがありますか。

たんご

かていか	home science	かつどう	activity
こてん	classical Japanese	ちがいます <ちがう>	be different
せいぶつ	biology	せんたく	elective, selection
せかいし	world history	にています <にている>	be similar
ぶつり	physics	やりかた	how to do
ほけん	health		
りんり	ethics		
OCB	oral communication		

さちこさんのオーストラリアの高校の時間わり

Read Sachiko's Australian timetable and write in Japanese how it differs from the timetable at her school in Japan, and your school timetable.

私の 10 年生の時間わり

	月	火	水	木	金
1 8:45–9:40	すうがく	英語	すうがく	れきし	りか
2 9:40–10:35	ちり	びじゅつ	りか	英語	すうがく
中間休み					
3 10:55–11:50	ほけん たいいく	ちり	れきし	日本語	日本語
4 11:50–12:45	英語	たいいく	びじゅつ	れきし	ちり
ひる休み					
5 13:45–15:20	りか	日本語	スポーツ	びじゅつ	たいいく

れい

さちこさんの日本の高校の時間わりはとてもちがいます。日本では 14 のかもくを勉強していましたがオーストラリアでは 8 つのかもくをべんきょうしています。

Kanji	Reading	Meaning		A way to remember
食	た (べます) た (べる) ショク	to eat, food		Lift the lid of the tureen and you will see the food to **eat**.
飯	ハン	cooked rice, a meal		On the left food, on the right 反 han (the sound of this kanji). A bowl full of **rice**.
先	さき セン	ahead, previous, former		You can see the relay runner. He has gone **ahead** through the finishing ribbon.
外	そと ガイ	outside, foreign		**Outside** you can see the new moon at night and a flag pole.
前	まえ ゼン	in front, before		The moon is **in front** of a ram's horns mounted on the roof. It looks **ri** リ markable.
私	わたし シ	I, private		A tree 木 with a leaf falling off. **I** am a chip off the old block. Plus katakana ム I'm u …!
休	やす (み) やす (みます) やす (む) キュウ	holiday to rest, be absent		A person 人 **resting** under a tree 木.
宿	やど シュク	an inn, a lodging		A roof , a person 人, and 100 百. It cost ¥100 to stay in this **inn**.
題	ダイ	a title, a heading		The sun 日 over a roll of cloth 疋 and a big shell 貝. The **title** is 'The sun rolled the cloth under the shell'.

Compounds

How many meanings can you guess?

AB 36

ご飯	ごはん	先生	せんせい	名前	なまえ
夏休み	なつやすみ	冬休み	ふゆやすみ	外国	がいこく
昼休み	ひるやすみ	休日	きゅうじつ	宿題	しゅくだい

たんご

おかし	sweets	～かた	way of …	ばいてん	canteen/tuckshop
おやつ	snacks	がんばって!	don't give in	まちがえました	made a mistake
ぎょうぎがわるい	bad manners	ぐうぐう	zzzz! zzzz!	やっと	finally
キンコンカンコン	ting-a-ling	ねむい	sleepy	よごします	to stain

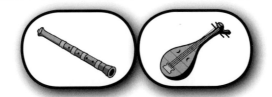

Take turns to be びわ and しゃくはち.

びわ: You are a Japanese exchange student. You are to go with your class to school adventure camp. You have never camped in the bush before and don't know what to expect.

First, find about the daily routine from しゃくはち, who is the camp leader.

What time do you have to get up and go to bed. Will there be any sport? Will you be going hiking?

Using the pictures, ask しゃくはち questions about what you need to take and what is allowed in the camp. Read the example conversation below.

しゃくはち: You are the camp leader of a school adventure camp. びわ is a Japanese exchange student who is coming to the camp with this class. You have given a talk to all the students explaining what they can take and what the rules are. Now you have to help びわ to understand what is expected.

In your notebook write down:

- the times they are to get up and go to bed
- what sport, if any, will be played
- what kinds of activities they will do. Choose from abseiling, hiking, swimming, climbing mountains, canoeing.

Using the pictures above decide which items are not permitted, which are essential and which are allowed. Answer びわ's questions.

⬭ れい

びわ:	キャンプで何時におきなければなりませんか。
しゃくはち:	５時半におきなければなりません。
びわ:	好きなたべものを もっていってもいいですか。
しゃくはち:	いいえ、たべものは もっていってはいけません。みんなで りょうりします。
びわ:	スニーカーをはいてもいいですか。
しゃくはち:	はい、いいです。スニーカーをはかなければなりません。

チェックしましょう 41

まんが – ジョンくんとスリッパ 1

あがります ＜上がる＞	to come/go up
あとで (あとに)	afterwards, later
いれます ＜いれる＞	to put in, insert
げたばこ	shoe cupboard
こちら	this way, here
つかれます ＜つかれる＞	to be tired
にもつ	luggage, baggage
ぬぎます ＜ぬぐ＞	to remove, take off
はこびます ＜はこぶ＞	to carry, transport
ようこそ	welcome

まんが – ジョンくんとスリッパ 2

あんないします ＜する＞	to guide, show around
ごめんなさい	I'm sorry
すみません	excuse me, thank you
ふくざつ (な)	complicated
ろうか	corridor, hallway

第一高校の校則

そめます ＜そめる＞	to dye
ちこくをします ＜する＞	to be late

レッドヒル高校の校則

アクセサリー	accessories (jewellery)
かぶります ＜かぶる＞	to wear (on the head)
かみます ＜かむ＞	to chew
くみ	a set, counter for sets
(お) けしょう	make-up, cosmetics
ごみ	rubbish
ごみばこ	rubbish bin
たばこをすいます ＜すう＞	to smoke
ピアス	earrings (pierced)
ピアスをします ＜する＞	to pierce the ear, to wear pierced earrings
ふくそう	appearance, dress code
マニキュア	manicure, nail polish
らくがき	graffiti

I can:
- behave appropriately in a Japanese home
- understand a polite Japanese welcome
- say someone is obliged to do something
- apologise and accept apologies
- tell someone not to do something
- understand and write school rules
- understand advice to exchange students
- understand and write a school timetable
- recognise and write the following kanji

食　飯　先　外　前　私　休　宿　題

かていせいかつと お祝い
いわ
Family life and celebrations

part 2

In these three units you will learn how to:
- recognise formal and informal language
- speak informally
- write a diary
- express feelings and opinions
- read a recipe
- make comparisons
- express giving and receiving
- talk about family life in Japan and Australia
- talk about celebrations in Japan and Australia.

Contents

はずかしかった こと
Embarrassing events

ジョンくんの日記

Diaries are always written in plain (informal) style because writers are writing for themselves and there is no need to be respectful.

Japanese diaries have either blank pages or spaces like this for the

___ 月　　___ 日　　___ 曜日　　　天気 ___

month　　date　　　day of the week　　and weather　　to be entered.

AB 45(1)

> 12月10日　　水曜日　天気　はれ
>
> あさ、9時半に なりたに ついた.
> まだ はやくて とても さむかった.
> くうこうで ホストファミリーに あった.
> みんな とても やさしくて ぼくは
> ラッキーだ. うちについて、まず、
> おばあさんに じこしょうかいを した.
> せいこう！ でも くつを ぬがなかった.
> しっぱい！ いえの中では スリッパを
> はかなくちゃ. ろうかを トイレの
> スリッパで あるいた. しっぱい‼
> あーあ、 いえのきそくは とても
> ふくざつだ！ ぼく、だいじょうぶかな？
> しんぱいだ……．

わかりましたか

1 Can you find the plain form of the following verbs in John's diary?
   a ぬぎませんでした
   b つきました
   c あいました
   d はいりました
   e はかなければなりません
2 Can you find an example of the plain form of です?
3 Can you find the expressions used for:
   • blunder?
   • success?
4 What do you think 「ワァー！」means?
5 Why is it written in katakana?

First night in Japan

AB 45(2)

Japanese is increasingly absorbing foreign words, especially English words. This sometimes leads to misunderstandings, as in the cartoon above.

る、おふろに はいったが びっくりした。
おゆが すごくあつくて「ワァー!」 水をたくさんいれて
いった。 きもちが よかった。 あ～～～.
ぎの人が おふろに はいって、
「ワァ! ジョンさん!」 「……?」
おゆが ない! おふろが きたない.」
え?…あ! いけない! ごめんなさい!」
ふろの中で、 せっけんをつかっては いけない. それに
ふろの おゆを ながしては いけない. しっぱい、しっぱい!

わかりましたか

1 Can you find these expressions?
 a The hot water was extremely hot and …
 b You shouldn't use soap in the bath.
 c You shouldn't let out the hot water.
2 Can you make a rule for forming the plain past of い ending adjectives?

18 How to make the plain past of verbs

The plain past

Think of the て form of the verb (see page 184) and change て to た.

う verbs	かいます	かって	かった	bought
	かきます	かいて	かいた	wrote
	およぎます	およいで	およいだ	swam
	はなします	はなして	はなした	spoke
	たちます	たって	たった	stood
	しにます	しんで	しんだ	died
	あそびます	あそんで	あそんだ	had fun, played
	よみます	よんで	よんだ	read
	のります	のって	のった	boarded, rode
	*いきます	いって	いった	went
る verbs	たべます	たべて	たべた	ate
	みます	みて	みた	saw
irregular verbs	きます	きて	きた	came
	します	して	した	did

The plain past negative

You have already studied the plain present/future negative in Unit 2 (page 23).
See also page 183.

Change ない to なかった.

う verbs	かいます	かわない	かわなかった	did not buy
	かきます	かかない	かかなかった	did not write
	およぎます	およがない	およがなかった	did not swim
	はなします	はなさない	はなさなかった	did not speak
	たちます	たたない	たたなかった	did not stand
	しにます	しなない	しななかった	did not die
	あそびます	あそばない	あそばなかった	did not play
	よみます	よまない	よまなかった	did not read
	のります	のらない	のらなかった	did not ride
る verbs	たべます	たべない	たべなかった	did not eat
	みます	みない	みなかった	did not watch
irregular verbs	きます	* こない	こなかった	did not come
	します	しない	しなかった	did not do

*exception

19 How to make the plain past of adjectives and nouns

> Remove です after the past form of い ending adjectives (positive and negative).

です after い ending adjectives has no meaning. It is used to make the sentence more polite. Removing です makes the sentence informal and so less polite.

れい

はずかしかった~~です~~	はずかしかった	was embarrassed, shy
よかった~~です~~	よかった	was good
さむくなかった~~です~~	さむくなかった	was not cold
たかくなかった~~です~~	たかくなかった	was not expensive

> Change でした to だった after な adjectives and nouns (positive).
> Remove です after な adjective and nouns (negative).

In the case of な adjectives and nouns the でした does have meaning. It is there to convey the idea of the past tense as well as to make the sentence polite. The plain form of でした is だった.

れい

ふくざつ~~でした~~	ふくざつだった	was complicated
先生~~でした~~	先生だった	was a teacher
しずかじゃなかった~~です~~	しずかじゃなかった	was not quiet
いしゃじゃなかった~~です~~	いしゃじゃなかった	was not a doctor

For a summary of adjectives see page 187.

20 The plain form of です

		Polite	Plain (informal)
is		です	だ
was		でした	だった
is not	formal	ではありません	
		ではないです	ではない
	polite	じゃないです	じゃない
was not	formal	ではありませんでした	ではなかった
		ではなかったです	
	polite	じゃなかったです	じゃなかった

1 Japanese exchange students じろう and けいこ are explaining what they did last weekend. Try to write their diary in Japanese, using plain form. **AB** 50

「しゅうまつに何をしましたか。」

じろう

えーと、ぼくはホストファミリーの家族と山に行きました。テントを はって、バーベキューをしました。とても おいしかったです。それから、川で さかなつりも しました。よるは キャンプ・ファイヤーをしました。ほしがきれいでした。

けいこ

私は、ともだちといっしょにかいものに行きました。コアラの T シャツと えはがきをかいました。とてもあつかったです。だから、ともだちとアイスクリームを食べました。とても 大きくて、びっくりしました。よる、日本の家族に えはがきをかきました。

2 Write a diary account of what you did yesterday. Write in plain form. If you keep a regular diary in Japanese, you will be practising the plain form and reinforcing the language you are learning.

イディオム

かな is an interjection used to express feelings. Depending on the situation it can express feeling of concern such as: I wonder; I guess; I dare say; alas; or asking for agreement in a similar way to ね. Also, it is often used when talking to oneself, and is often lengthened to かなあ.

（れい）

ぼく（は）だいじょうぶかな…   I wonder if I will be okay.

かれは 食べてみたかな…   I guess he tried to eat it.

It can also be similar in meaning to 'eh':

（れい）

できるかな？   You can do it, eh?

もう食べたかな？   You have eaten, eh?

How to express your feelings

1 うれしい

2 かなしい

3 はずかしい

4 うらやましい

5 たのしい

6 さびしい

More about feelings

1 すごい

2 ざんねん
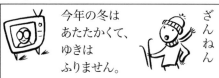

3 びっくりした

4 かわいそう

5 しかたがない

6 たいへん

わかりましたか

Study all the pictures on the page and decide which express:

- surprise
- admiration
- happiness
- loneliness
- resignation
- sympathy, pity
- sadness
- enjoyment
- envy
- embarrassment
- regret, disappointment
- horror.

Weather

These weather expressions are used at the top of each day's diary entry.

 雨
あめ

 雪
ゆき

晴れ
は

曇り
くも

Other expressions are usually used within the diary entry when commenting on the weather.

 むしあつい

すずしい

あたたかい

風が つよい
かぜ

わかりましたか

1 Can you find the plain present of the following verbs in Sachiko's diary?

a あけます

b つきます

c あります

d かざります

e します

f むかえます

g いいます

h まっています

2 Can you find the expressions used for the following?

a Put a Christmas tree in the house.

b I wonder what my present will be.

c The lights are turned on.

d Beautifully decorated.

AB 45(1)

CD1
track 22–23

12月25日　木曜日　天気　くもり

今日は クリスマス。 オーストラリアでは
みんな いえの 中に クリスマスツリーを
おいて、花や いろいろな デコレーション
で いえの 中を きれいに かざる。 とても
きれいだ。 よるは スイッチ、オン！ ……
ツリーに ライトが つく。 赤、青、みどり、
ああ、とても ロマンチック……。
けさは、子どもは みんな はやく おきて
まっている。 あー、もうすぐ プレゼントを
あける。 日本の クリスマスより ずっといい
なぁ……。 私の プレゼントは 何かなあ？
はやく 見たい。 大きい プレゼント、
小さい プレゼント、いろいろ ある。

わかりましたか

1 Read Sachiko's diary for 31 December. In your notebook, indicate if the the following statements are TRUE (T), FALSE (F) or NOT KNOWN (NK).

   a   In Japan New Year's Eve is called Oshogatsu.
   b   People drink cool drinks because the weather is hot and humid
   c   The party starts at 12 o'clock.
   d   Sachiko is feeling happy because everyone hugged and kissed her.
   e   There is a lot of hooting at 12 o'clock.
   f   Sachiko is surprised by the hooting.
   g   Sachiko has mixed feelings about the New Year's Eve party.

2 Find these expressions.

   a   Hug each other.
   b   I was surprised.
   c   Everyone ate various things, etc.
   d   Exactly at 12 o'clock.
   e   Welcome in the New Year.
   f   How embarrassing!

3 Guess which song ほたるのひかり is in English.

幸子さんの日記   AB 45(2)
さち　　　　にっき

12月31日　水曜日　天気 雨

おおみそかは、ニュー・イヤーズ・イブ という。
よるは 12時まで パーティー を する。
こんやも、とても むしあついが、空に
ほしが たくさん 見える。
みんな いろいろな ものを 食べたり、
つめたい のみものを のんだりしている。
そして、ちょうど 12時に ほたるの ひかりの
うたを うたって、あたらしい 年を むかえる。
みんな 「ハッピー・ニュー・イヤー！」と
言って、キスしたり、だきあったりする。
私は びっくり！ ああ、はずかしい。
私も 一人に キスした。また、つぎの
人に キスした。
ああ、はずかしい……。

21 How to make the plain/present/future of verbs

Present/future tense (dictionary form)

う verbs	Take off ます. Change the previous vowel sound from an い sound to the corresponding う sound on the hiragana chart (see page 182).

れい

かいます	かい	かう	to buy
いります	いり	いる	to need
あります	あり	ある	to exist, to be, to have (inanimate)

For a complete explanation see pages 181 and 185.

る verbs	Take off ます. Add る.

れい

たべます	たべる	to eat
おしえます	おしえる	to teach
います	いる	to exist, to be, to have (animate)

How to tell the difference between う verbs and る verbs

Most る verbs have an 'e' sound before ます.

A few verbs have an 'i' sound so could be confused with う verbs. These few include common verbs such as みます (see), います (be), きます (wear), おきます (get up), できます (can do) and しんじます (believe).

irregular	します	する	to do
verbs	きます	くる	to come

This is your schedule for next week. Choose an activity for each day from the list provided and complete the schedule. Write in plain form, in your notebook.

月	AM	
	PM	へやをそうじ しなければならない
火	AM	ヘアカットをする
	PM	
水	AM	
	PM	友だちのパーティーに行く
木	AM	おじさんの うちへ 行く
	PM	
金	AM	
	PM	アルバイトをする ($45)
土	AM	
	PM	ベビーシッターをする ($26)
日	AM	
	PM	

- パーティのへやを花でかざります。
- DVD をかります。
- プレゼントをかいます。
- ともだちと DVD をみます。
- 日本語をべんきょうしなければなりません。
- 父とじょうばをします。
- 兄とゆうえんちであそびます。
- 日本人のペンパルに手紙をかきます。
- ほうかご、スポーツをします。

キャンプで

You are at a school camp in Japan. The teacher is giving you tomorrow's schedule. Write the following times in your notebook and fill in your schedule.

CD1
track 24

6.00	3.00
7.00	4.00
8.00	5.00
9.00	6.00
10.00	7.00
11.00	8.00
12.00	9.00
1.00	10.00
2.00	11.00

22 How to say 'It is called 〜.'

'It is called 〜.'

name	と	いいます。

'What is it called?'

〜 は	何と	いいますか。

れい

おおみそかは 英語で ニュー・イヤーズ・イブという。

Oomisoka is called New Year's Eve in English.

さっぽろの 冬のまつりは 何といいますか。

What is the winter festival in Sapporo called?

雪まつりといいます。

It is called the Snow Festival.

This といいます (is called) is usually written in hiragana, not kanji.

1　Answer these questions.

a 'rules' は 日本語で、何といいますか。

b 'Students studying abroad' は 日本語で、何といいますか。

c まつりは えい語で、何といいますか。

d じょうばは えい語で、何といいますか。

e お正月は えい語で、何といいますか。
　　しょうがつ

2　Make questions and answers using the words below.

a luggage

b hobby

c uniform

d どくしょ

e 外国

f やさい

23 How to quote what someone says or said

Person は	sentence in plain form	と	言っています。	says that
	sentence in plain form	と	言っていました。	said that
		と	言いました。	

Note: In direct speech, the speaker's utterance is placed in quotation marks.

The tense of 言う and what is quoted do not have to be the same.

(れい)

よし子さんは 「あしたも いっしょに えいがを みに行く？」と 言いました。

Yoshiko said, 'Shall we go to the movies together tomorrow as well?'

みんな ハッピー・ニュー・イヤーと 言って いる。

Everyone says 'Happy New Year'

さちこさんは はずかしい と言っていた。

Sachiko said 'How embarrassing.'

ジョンさんは きそくは ふくざつだ と言っている。

John says that the rules are complicated.

さちこさんは みんなおかしを食べている と言った。

Sachiko said that everyone was (is) eating sweets.

さちこさんは わからないと 言った。

Sachiko said that she did not understand.

…と言っていました is usually used to express 'said that'.

…と言いました is usually used in story telling and essays.

…と言っています is usually used for the present tense, not と言います。

---

1   Ben has just come back from Japan. Tell your friends what Ben said.

日本の冬は たいへん さむかったです。

ホストファミリーは とても しんせつでした。

日本の食べものは おいしかったです。

でも さしみは あまり 好きじゃないです。

しんかんせんに のりました。

しんかんせんは すごく はやくはしります。

きょうとで 学校に 行きました。

2   Using John's and Sachiko's diaries, create a dialogue in which you quote what each of them said about their experiences.

24 Doing this, that and the other and so on

| verb た form | + り | verb た form | + り + します。

します。
しました。
して すごしました。　I spent the time doing.
して たのしみました。I enjoyed doing.

Use this form when:

1   you want to list several activities but not everything, and the order is not important (the particle や is used in similar cases with nouns)

> れい
>
> およいだり、テニスをしたり します。
>
> We swim, play tennis and so on.
>
> テレビを 見たり、ゲームをしたり しました。
>
> We watched TV and played games, among other things.
>
> 食べたり、のんだり、あそんだり して、すごしました。
>
> We spent the time doing such things as eating drinking and having fun.
>
> DVD を 見たり して、たのしみました。
>
> We enjoyed ourselves watching DVDs, among other things.

2   two opposite movements are expressed: going up and down, coming and going, turn on and off.

> れい
>
> クリスマスツリーのライトがついたり、きえたりしていました。
>
> The Christmas tree lights were blinking on and off.
>
> 今日は 雨が ふったり、やんだり して、へんな 天気です。
>
> It is funny weather today—it rains on and off.

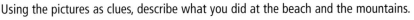

Using the pictures as clues, describe what you did at the beach and the mountains.

Kanji	Reading	Meaning		A way to remember
赤	あか(い) セキ	red		土 (Saturday) over 小 (small) katakana ノ (no). **Red** no(se) day on Saturday is to help small people.
青	あお(い) セイ	blue, blue-green, fresh		生 (being born—without ノ) + 月 moon. A **blue** new-born moon.
空	そら クウ	sky, air		Under the sky ⌒ the air streams down. Katakana エ for E–r (air).
雪	ゆき セツ	snow		雨 (rain) over katakana ヨ (yo). **Snow** falls when rain piles up like yoghurt.
曜	ヨウ	day of the week		日 (day) next to ヨヨ (yo for the sound) over a bird. On the first **day** a partridge in a pear tree, etc.
花	はな カ	flower		⺾ (the sign for a plant) over 人 (person) + katakana ヒ. He gives a **flower** to a person.
間	カン あいだ	period of time, during		The sun 日 appears to move between the gates 門 as it measures **periods of time**.

Compounds

AB 48

How many meanings can you guess?

赤ちゃん	あかちゃん	赤土	あかつち	青年	せいねん
青春	せいしゅん	雪水	ゆきみず	花火	はなび
時間	じかん	日曜日	にちようび	青空	あおぞら
空中	くうちゅう	空気	くうき	空港	くうこう

おこのみやきを食べた

Try making this dish.

12月14日　　　　日曜日　　天気　雨のちはれ

きのうは、とてもさむくて雪がふったりやんだりしていた。はじめて雪を見た。けさは雪が雨にかわってざんねんだった。でもごごから空がはれてあたたかくなった。青い空が見えて、うれしくなった。

ばんご飯に、みんなでおこのみやきをつくった。おこのみやきは、テーブルにホットプレートをおいて、目の前でやいて食べる。とてもたのしくて、おいしかった。またつくりたいから、ここにざいりょうとつくりかたをメモする。おこのみやきのしゃしんもスキャンする。

ざいりょう

こむぎこ　1/2カップ　キャベツ(こまかくきる)　1カップ
たまご　1こ　にく(うすくきる)　100g(えびやいかでもいい)
水　1/4カップ　しょうゆ、コンソメ、マヨネーズ、ウスターソース

つくりかた

1　ボールに、こむぎこと、たまごと水とコンソメ、しょうゆをいれて、よくまぜる。
2　1にキャベツをいれる。
3　ホットプレートをあつくして、オイルをいれて、2をやく。
　　その上、にくをおく。
　　りょうめん、やく
　　マヨネーズやソースをかけて食べる。
　　お母さんは、かつおぶしと青のりをかけて食べていた。

たんご

青のり	seaweed sprinkles	かつおぶし	bonito flakes
いか	squid	キャベツ	cabbage
えび	prawns	コンソメ	chicken cube
かわる	to change	スキャンする	to scan
こむぎこ	flour	つくりかた	how to make
ざいりょう	ingredients	まぜる	to mix
たまご	egg	やく	to pan-fry
ホットプレート	electric fry pan	マヨネーズ	mayonnaise
りょうめん	both sides		

おやこどんぶりをつくろう！

おやこどんぶりのレシピ
Try making this dish.

ざいりょう

とりにく	500 g
たまねぎ (中)	2 こ
にんじん (中)	1 本
だし	3 カップ
たまご	4 こ
ねぎ	1 本
しょうゆ、さとう、しお	少々
のり	1 まい
ごはん	ちゃわんに 4 はい

つくりかた

1　とりにく、たまねぎ、にんじんを こまかく きる。
2　なべに だし、しょうゆ、さとう、しおをいれて、あつくする。
3　2 の中に 1 をいれて、五分ぐらいにる。
4　ときたまごを、3 の中にいれる。
5　あついごはんの上に 4 をのせる。スープもすこしかける。
6　ねぎとのりを小さくきって、上にのせて、できあがり！

たんご

だし	soup stock	たまねぎ	onion
できあがり	be ready	ときたまご	beaten egg
とりにく	chicken	なべ	soup pan
にんじん	carrot	にる	cook
のせる	place on	ねぎ	shallots
のり	nori seaweed		

日本のテーブルマナー

「いただきます。」と「ごちそうさま。」を言わなければなりません。

ごはんのおちゃわんと、みそしるの おわんはもって食べましょう。

自分のおさらにとって 食べなければなりません。

ひじをついて食べてはいけません。

おはしのつかいかた

食べ物をつきさしてはいけません。

おはしであそんではいけません。

おはしで食器（しょっき）をひきよせてはいけません。

人のおはしから、おはしで食べ物をとってはいけません。

わかりましたか

Read the article about table manners and indicate whether the following behaviours are considered polite when dining with a Japanese family.

a   You move a dish or plate by using your chopsticks.

b   You hold a rice bowl and soup bowl when you eat.

c   You take as much as you can eat onto your individual plate when the dish is served in a communal dish.

d   You use your chopsticks to take food from someone else's chopsticks.

e   You eat with your elbows on the table.

すごくはずかしい

Listen to John's embarrassing story. Make a list of his mistakes.

CD1
track 25

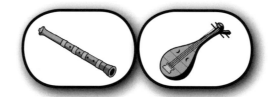

Take turns to be しゃくはち and びわ.

しゃくはち: Choose one of the situations from the following list and a suitable feeling from the illustrations below.

Tell びわ your choice of situation and when asked how you feel about it try to keep a conversation going. Use the example as a guide.

1 テストがおわった。

2 こんばん、パーティーに行く。

3 ともだちのお父さんはあたらしい車を買った。

4 ともだちがほかの学校に行った。

5 今日、お母さんが学校の前でキスした。

びわ: Listen to what しゃくはち says. Ask how (s)he feels about it. Try to guess. Keep the conversation going.

（れい）

しゃくはち:	テストがおわった。
びわ:	どんなきもち？　うれしい？
しゃくはち:	うれしくない。
びわ:	じゃ、かなしい？
しゃくはち:	いいえ、かなしくない。
びわ:	じゃ、ざんねん？
しゃくはち:	うん、よくできなかったから、とてもざんねんだよ。

チェックしましょう

ジョンくんの日記

しっぱい	blunder, mistake
すごく	awfully, extremely
せいこう	success
せっけん	soap
ながします <ながす> ⑦	to drain, let flow
びっくりします <する>	to be surprised
(お) ふろ	bath
まず	first of all
(お) ゆ	hot water

日本のテーブルマナー

(お) さら	plate
しょっき(食器)	tableware
じぶん(自分)の	one's own
(お) ちゃわん、わん	bowl
つきさします <つきさす> ⑦	to stick, pierce
(お) はし	chopsticks
ひきよせます <ひきよせる> ⑤	bring closer
ひじをつきます <つく> ⑦	rest elbow on
みそしる	miso soup

幸子さんの日記

おおみそか	New Year's Eve
キスをします <する>	to kiss
クリスマスツリー	Christmas tree
けさ	this morning
こんや	this evening, tonight
スイッチ・オン	switch on
だきあいます <だきあう> ⑦	to hug each other
ちょうど	exactly, precisely
つきます <つく> ⑦	to be turned on
デコレーション	decoration
ニュー・イヤーズ・イブ	New Year's Eve
はずかしい	embarrassed
ほし	stars
むしあつい	hot and humid
もうすぐ	soon
～より	than ~

I can:
- read and write a journal entry in plain form
- express my feelings
- describe the weather
- make notes in plain form
- say what something is called
- quote what someone said or says
- list what I did or will do
- understand and follow a recipe
- understand Japanese table manners
- recognise and write the following kanji
  赤 青 空 雪 曜 花 見

CD1
track 27-30

日本での休み
Holidays in Japan

Unit 5

クリスマスの買い物 (かいもの)

イディオム

用 (よう) means 'use'. It is commonly used in shopping situations.

れい

子供用 (こどもよう) for children
　(for children's use)
おとな用 for adults
ペット用 for pets
プレゼント用 for a present

Note: ハローキティ
Hello Kitty is a cartoon figure very popular with young girls. It appears on all kinds of merchandise such as notepaper, rulers, erasers and clothing.

かいわ1

いらっしゃいませ。

えっと、ハンカチはどこですか。

はい、こちらです。いろいろないろがありますが・・・・。

そうですね。ぜんぶきれいないろですね。これはいくらですか。

1まい、500円です。

じゃあ、この青いのと、この白いのと、ピンクのと、3まいください。

はい、かしこまりました。1500円になります。

じゃあ、これ、2000円。

ありがとうございます。500円のおつりです。

はい、どうも。あのう、子ども用のTシャツは何階ですか。

Tシャツは3階です。

かいわ2

いらっしゃいませ。何かおさがしですか。

ええ。子供用のTシャツをさがしています。

男の子用ですか、女の子用ですか。

女の子のです。

何才用ですか。

その子は10才ですけど・・・。

大きいお子さんですか。

いいえ、そんなに大きくないです。

そうですか・・・。こちらにいろいろなキャラクターのTシャツがありますが、いかがですか。

ああ、その子はハローキティが大好きです。これはいくらですか。

そちらは2600円です。

うわっ、ちょっと高いなあ。でも、クリスマスプレゼントだから・・・。それにします。プレゼント用につつんでください。

はい、かしこまりました。

いらっしゃいませ。プレゼントですか。

ええ、ちょっとお父さんに……。ゴルフが好きだから、ゴルフボールはどうかな。

これはいかがですか。タイガー・ウッズのブランドのボールです。今とても人気がありますよ。

えっ？タイガー・ウッズ？かっこいいなあ。でも、いくらですか。

6こで３０００円です。

そうかあ。ねだんがちょっと……。

こちらはいかがですか。ゴルフボール6こと、スポーツタオルのセットで２０００円ですが。

ああ、いいですね。それにします。

はい、ありがとうございます。

いらっしゃいませ。

すみませんが、ちょっと、そのスカーフを見せて下さい。

こちらですか。

いいえ、そのとなりの花がらのです。

ああ、こちらですね。はい、どうぞ。

きれいですね。

はい、こちらはフランスのディオールのデザインです。

いくらですか。

９０００円です。

そうですか。えっと……。

こちらのはいかがですか。日本のわかいデザイナーのもので、２５００円です。シルクですから、あたたかいですよ。

いいですね。これにします。じゃ、これ、３０００円。

ありがとうございます。５００円のおつりです。

わかりましたか

1 Guess the meaning of かしこまりました。
2 What items did John buy for the family?
3 If the exchange rate was ¥70 = $1, how much did he pay for the presents?

25 Making decisions in shops and restaurants

noun	に	します (する)

れい

それにします	I will have that one.
このハンカチにします	I will have this handkerchief.
すしにします	I will have the sushi.

Choose from the following and say which you have decided on.

26 Talking about things without naming them

い adjective	の
な adjective	なの

れい

赤いのが ありますか。	Do you have a red one?
青いのを ください。	The blue one please.
そのきれいなのは いくらですか。	How much is that pretty one?

The language of sales assistants

Shop assistants use very polite language called *keigo*. You will learn more about this in *Mirai 6*.

Here is a list of the expressions used in the dialogues on pages 66 and 67.

いらっしゃいませ	This expression is used to welcome customers.
こちら	This means 'here' and is the formal form of ここ and これ.
そちら	This means 'there' and is the formal form of そこ and それ.
なにかおさがしですか。	This means 'Are you looking for something?'.
かしこまりました。	This expression is the equivalent of 'Certainly Sir/Madam'.

Matsuya Ginza

ゴルフテラス ペット プレイグラウンド	ペット用品 _{ようひん}	ゴルフスクール「オン・ザ・グリーン」		R
レストラン	ミスタードーナツ カレーハウス	ピザパーラー アイスクリームパーラー	すしバー おそばや	7
リビング	デザインコレクション デザインギャラリー	ギフトサロン ナイトウェア	タオル リビングアクセサリー	6
子供 _{こども} スポーツ	学生服 _{がくせいふく} ゴルフ用品 スポーツシューズ メガネ	ボーイスカウトショップ ベビー・子供服 _{こどもふく} アウトドア用品	クラフトギャラリー スイムウェア ミスターミニット	5
紳士服 _{しんしふく} 「スーツ」	スーツ・ジャケット・スラックス・コート　ジーンズ フォーマル・ワイシャツ・ネクタイ　　メンズコンセプトショップ			4
婦人服 _{ふじんふく} 「ミセス・イン ポート」	インターナショナル・デザイナーズ・サロン ベルト　フォーマル　　　コート　ハンカチ　キャッシュサービス セーター　ブラウス　　フォトスタジオ　カフェ			3
婦人服 「キャリア」	デザイナーズ・スポーツウェア　スモールサイズ　カードセンター アクセサリー　　　　　　ハンドバッグ　　スカーフ ランジェリー　　　　キャリアスポーツウェア			2
婦人服 「ヤング」	ヤングカジュアル　　フラワーショップ　　カフェ&レストラン			1
食品 _{しょくひん}	パン おかし	和洋酒 _{わようしゅ}	フルーツ　　　コーヒーショップ カフェ	B1
生鮮食品 _{せいせんしょくひん}	鮮魚 _{せんぎょ}	精肉 _{せいにく}	アイスクリームとジュースバー くすり	B2
地下鉄連絡口 _{ちかてつれんらくぐち}	野菜 _{やさい}	つけ物 _{もの}	喫茶店 _{きっさてん}	

わかりましたか

John wants to buy:

- some handkerchiefs for Obaasan
- a scarf for Okaasan
- a T-shirt for Makoto
- some golf balls for Otoosan
- some sweets for Reiko
- a bunch of flowers for Okaasan
- some Christmas cards
- a cold drink
- some tennis shoes for himself.

On which floors will he find these items?

1 Find the plain forms that match the following polite forms.

a かわいい ですね。

b かわなければ なりません。

c どうしましたか。(What is the matter?)

d おかしい ですね。

e きらいでは ありません。

f どうして プレゼントが ありませんか。

g かいます。

h お金です。

i ちょきん します。

3 Match the following expressions in the cartoon story.

a Isn't it cute!

b Wow! It looks delicious.

c What's up?

d That's the lot. Mum's, Dad's, Makoto's and Reiko's.

e I will eat it for you.

f Well, anyway, here are the presents.

g It is strange.

h Happy New Year!

i Why didn't I get any presents?

j I am going to save the money.

k Computer game.

l I want to become rich.

m It will soon be Christmas.

n Everyone can buy what they like.

2 How are these interjections expressed in the cartoon?

a Um!

b Wow!

c Come now.

d Hmm.

e Really?

f Er …

g Let's see.

h Heh!

i Ah!

j Yippee!

k What?

l Eh?

> **Hint:**
> ええっと、
> ふーん、
> え?
> へえー、
> あっ、
> さあ、
> ああ、
> わあ、
> うわー、
> うっ!
> ええ、
> ヤッホー!

おとしだま

a present of money given to all the children of the family at New Year. New notes are always used.

27 Saying how things appear   AB 61

adjective い̶	+ そう (です)
adjective な	+ そう (です)
verb ま̶す̶	

れい

たのしそう (です)　looks enjoyable

元気そう (です)　looks well

よさそう (です)　looks good

あめが ふりそう (です)　looks like rain

Adjectives such as きれい and うつくしい which describe appearance are not used with そうです.

28 Using informal speech

When? When talking to close friends and classmates, to host brothers and sisters and to yourself you use informal speech.

Why? Informal speech does not show deference to the person addressed so it allows you to sound warm and friendly. The use of the *masu*/*desu* forms to classmates and close friends can make you sound distant and reserved.

If you use informal speech to people who are not close friends—such as teachers, people who are senior to you, shop assistants, taxi drivers—you will sound rude and brash.

In Japan, senior staff in offices and businesses use informal speech when speaking to juniors, so you would sound insulting if you use informal speech to the wrong people.

Characteristics of informal speech

1 The plain form of verbs and adjectives is used.
2 だ and だった are used instead of です and でした.
3 Words and particles are often omitted.
4 Particles such as よ, わ, の and かな are often added to the end of the sentence. わ is usually used only by females.
5 Questions are formed by:
   • a rising intonation alone, for example なに？ どこ？ 行く？ 行った？ 行かない？
   • the addition of の？ after verbs, for example どこへ行くの？ 行かないの？

いろいろなかいわ

Listen to the conversations. Write the number of each true statement below in your notebook.
(F = female, M = male)

CD1
track 33

1 a F and M are family members.
   b F and M are acquaintances.
   c M is F's senior.
2 a F and M are acquaintances.
   b F and M are friends.
   c M is F's boss.
3 a F and M have never met before.
   b F and M are classmates.
   c F and M are acquaintances.

4 a F barely knows M.
   b F is senior to M.
   c F is M's friend.
5 a F and M are acquaintances.
   b F and M are family members.
   c F and M are friends.

Change the following dialogue between acquaintances to a dialogue between friends.

なかむら： もしもし、いけださんですか。なかむらですけれど...。

いけだ： あ！ なかむらさん、こんにちは。

なかむら： こんにちは。ええと あしたの ごごは いそがしいですか。

いけだ： そうですね。あの... 3 時から ひまですけど...。

なかむら： じゃ、4 時にうちへ 来ませんか。ジョーンズさんとすずきさんも 来ますよ。ジョーンズさんは土曜日に アメリカへ かえりますから 4 人で 小さいパーティーを したいんです。

いけだ： それは いいですね。私しも 行きます。

29 Congratulations and good wishes

Birthday	お誕生日 たんじょうび	+	おめでとう (ございます)
New Year	あけまして	+	おめでとう (ございます)
Wedding	ご結婚 けっこん	+	おめでとう (ございます)
Christmas	メリー・クリスマス		
Mother's Day	お母さん、ありがとう		
Father's Day	お父さん、ありがとう		

hoping that this year will be a good one too

New Year greeting

the year of the rat

name and address and telephone number

漢字
かんじ

AB 59

Kanji	Reading	Meaning		A way to remember
正	ただ (しい) ショウ	correct, precise		止 (とまる) stop. See the line you should **stop** at __. This is the **correct** thing to do.
早	はや (い) ソウ	early		日 (the sun) will be up in 十 (10) minutes. It is **early**.
買	か(う) か(います) バイ	to buy		貝 (shells used for money) + an abacus to help you to **buy.**
週	シュウ	a week		土 (Saturday) over 口 (mouth) enclosed by part of Monday with a caterpillar. The **week** goes slowly.
朝	あさ チョウ	morning		日 (the sun) with two stars and 月 (the moon). It is **morning**.
来	く (る) き (ます) ライ	to come, coming		木 (tree) that is still a sapling. It has extra shoots at the top. It is **coming** out of the earth.
白	しろ (い) ハク	white		A seed is sprouting. A small **white** shoot is just showing.

Compounds

AB 60

How many meanings can you guess?

お正月	おしょうがつ	買い物	かいもの	来年	らいねん
来週	らいしゅう	来月	らいげつ	今朝	けさ
朝ご飯	あさごはん	朝食	ちょうしょく	早朝	そうちょう
白人	はくじん	白金	はっきん	白紙	はくし

お正月のかいわ
しょうがつ

AB 57

On the first day after the winter holidays, John meets someone.

Read or listen to the conversation that took place and complete the quiz on page 77.

すすむ： おはよう、ジョン！ お正月は どうだった？

ジョン： あ、すすむくん、おはよう！ うん、お正月は とてもおもしろかった！ お年だま、たくさん もらったよ。すすむくんは？

すすむ： お年だま？ 今年は ちょっと すくなかったねえ。は、は、は！ ジョンは お年だまで 何か買ったの？

ジョン： うん、ノーラ・ジョーンズの CD 買ったけど、日本は CD がとても 高いね！

すすむ： へえー、ジョンはノーラ・ジョーンズが好き？！ ぼくは ああいう おんがくはあまり 好きじゃないよ。ところで、お正月は どこへ 行ったの？

ジョン： まず、家族みんなで じんじゃへ はつもうでに 行ったんだけど、朝、すごーく 早くてね、まだ くらくて さむくて たいへんだったよ！ ねむかったけど 朝日を見て とっても 気もちがよかった！！

すすむ： へえー、はつもうでに 行ったの？！ ジョン、えらい！ やっぱりオーストラリア人は えらーい！ ぼくは ふとんの中で グーグーねむっていたからね。

ジョン： ひどいなあ。はつもうでから かえってね、みんなで 朝ご飯におぞうにを 食べたんだけど…

すすむ： おぞうに？ ああ、おもちは どうだった？

ジョン： まずい、まずい！ ガムだよ！ 口の中で だんだん 大きくなるんだよ。ほんとに こまった！

すすむ： は、は、は！ それで？ どうしたの？ 食べたの？

ジョン： ううん、それでね、てで、口の中から おもちを とりだしたんだけど…

すすむ： それで？ どうしたの？

ジョン： たいへんだった！！ てについて、ベタ ベタ ベタ…

すすむ： はっ はっ はっ！

わかりましたか

1 In your notebook, indicate if the following statements are TRUE (T), FALSE (F) or NOT KNOWN(NK). Write down the reason for your choice.

a The two are probably classmates because they are using informal speech.

b Susumu received lots of money at Oshoogatsu.

c John bought a Norah Jones CD with the money he received.

d Susumu is envious because he cannot afford to buy a Norah Jones CD.

e Susumu went to the shrine to pay his respects on the first day of the year.

f Susumu thinks that Australians are amazing.

g John thinks that Susumu is awful because he snores.

h John's family provided ozooni for breakfast.

i John thinks that ozooni is great.

j Susumu is laughing because John's teeth stuck together.

2 Can you guess why John says すごーく instead of すごく?

3 Can you guess why Susumu says えらーい instead of えらい?

4 What could ベタベタ mean?

おもち or もち

もち is rice cake, made from glutinous rice, which has a sticky consistency. After the rice has been steamed it is pounded in a mortar until it is smooth. Pounding the sticky rice requires strong muscles so this is usually done by male members of the family. The big lump of rice cake is then well floured and placed on a large tray that has also been well floured. Women and children pull off small pieces and mould it into flat round cakes with their hands.

Some big cakes are formed into large square sheets, which are cut into smaller square pieces after they harden. These can be stored for many days.

Rice cakes can be used in many ways. They can be cooked by grilling them on each side for a few minutes, or by boiling them briefly until they float. Freshly made rice cakes, sometimes with red bean paste inside, are often eaten while they are still soft.

もち is also used in a thick, sweet red-bean soup called ぜんざい. It can also be broiled and seasoned with soy sauce.

It is traditional to eat もち on New Year's Day served in おぞうに (clear soup).

おぞうに

ざいりょう

チキン、やさい、もち、
水、チキンコンソメ、
しょうゆ、しお

つくりかた

1　なべ (saucepan) に
　水とコンソメと チキンをいれる。
2　やさいを 小さく きる (cut)。
3　やさいを 1 のなべに いれる。
4　もちを くわえる (add)。
5　しょうゆと しおを くわえて 15 分、にる (simmer)

These days many people just buy もち at a shop.
Vacuum-packed もち is available all year round
at any supermarket.

30 Giving and receiving

Between other people, including family members

giver は	recipient に	thing を	あげます

れい

トムくんは スーさんに 本を あげます。
Tom gives a book to Sue.

recipient は	giver に or から	thing を	もらいます

れい

トムくんは スーさんに 本を もらいます。

Tom receives a book from Sue.

Note: Another verb やる (やります) also means 'to give'. It is used for giving things to animals, or to plants.

Between the speaker and others who are equal or junior, and family members

I/we は	recipient に	thing を	あげます

れい

私 (たち) は スーさんに 本を あげます。
I/we give a book to Sue.

recipient は	giver に or から	thing を	もらいます

れい

私 (たち) は スーさんに 本を もらいます。

I/we receive a book from Sue.

giver は/が	me/us に	thing を	くれます

れい

スーさんは/が 私 (たち) に 本を くれます。
Sue gives me/us a book.

The use of は or が after the giver will depend on the emphasis.

れい

スーさんは本をくれました。　　　Sue gave me a *book*.
スーさんが本をくれました。　　　*Sue* gave me a book.

Note: 私は and 私に are usually not needed if the meaning is clear.

Don't use あげます when you want to say that someone gives to you, the speaker.

Between the speaker and others who are senior to the speaker

I/we は	senior person に	thing を	さしあげます

れい

私 (たち) は 先生に 本を さしあげます。
I/we will give a book to the teacher

I/we は	senior person に or から	thing を	いただきます。

れい

私 (たち) は 先生に 本を いただきます。
I/we receive a book from the teacher.

senior person は/が	me/us に	thing を	くださいます。

れい

先生は/が 私 (たち) に 本を くださいます。
The teacher kindly gives me/us a book.

Note: If the speaker IS the senior person they will use あげます and もらいます。

れい

せいとに 本を あげました。   I gave a student a book.
せいとに/から この本をもらいました。   A student gave me this book.

れい

ドンくんがこれをくれました。   Don gave me this.
ドンくんがおとうとにこれをくれました。   Don gave this to my brother.
田中さんがそれをくださいました。   Mr Tanaka gave me that.
田中さんがともだちにそれをくださいました。   Mr Tanka gave my friend that.
じろうくんから手紙をもらいました。   I got a letter from Jiroo.
リー先生に手紙をいただきました。   I received a letter from Miss Lee.
母がリー先生に手紙をいただきました。   Mum received a letter from Miss Lee.
私はケンくんにえんぴつをあげました。   I gave Ken a pencil.
私は先生に花をさしあげました。   I gave some flowers to the teacher.

---

1 Express the following in Japanese.

  a I gave my friend a present.

  b My friend gave me a sandwich.

  c My Japanese teacher gave me a Japanese calendar.

  d I received a watch from my father.

  e Mum gave me a bicycle.

  f Toshi received a letter from Keiko.

  g I gave Miss Lee a present.

  h John gave Reiko some sweets.

2 What will you give your family and friends for their birthdays? Make a list following the example sentence.

れい　　　　　　　　　　　　　　　　　　　　　　　　　AB 62

私は 兄に Tシャツを あげます。

| 私は
ぼくは | 父
母
ボーイフレンド
ガールフレンド
先生 | に | ? | を | あげます。
さしあげます。 |

3 What did you receive for your last birthday? Make a list following the example sentence.

れい

私は 兄から 本を もらいました。

| 私は
ぼくは | お父さん
お母さん
ボーイフレンド
ガールフレンド
ピアノの先生 | から
or
に | ? | を | もらいました。
いただきました。 |

4 Using the diagram, say who gave you the following in two different ways.

れい

1 ドンさんが ペンを くれました。　　　**2** ドンさんにペンを もらいました。
　　先生が えはがきを くださいました。　　　　先生にえはがきを いただきました。

Mr Jones's mother, a present
Miss Lee (teacher), a dictionary

↓

My uncle,
this bicycle　　　　　　　　　　　　　　　　　　　　My friend John,
　　　　　　　　　　　　　　　　　　　　　　　　　　　a CD
My brother,　　　　　　　→　Me　←　　　　　　My mother,
that skateboard　　　　　　　　　　　　　　　this computer game

↑

My younger sister, a T-shirt
John's little brother, this photo

ジョンくんの手紙

A letter from John to his teacher and Year 11 Japanese class in Australia

先生、11 年生の みなさん、お元気ですか。日本では、今は 冬で、とても さむいです！ 時々 雪がふります！ はじめて、雪を 見ました。

ところで、日本の クリスマスは つまらなかったですよ。ホリデー じゃありませんでした！ ぼくは もちろん ホストファミリーの みなさんに プレゼントを買って あげました。でも、ぼくには だれも プレゼントを 買ってくれませんでした！ クリスマスの 朝、早く おきて まちましたが、とうとう 何も もらいませんでした。

よる、お父さんが クリスマス ケーキをかってきて くれました。でも、はこを あけて びっくりしました！ きれいな デコレーションの スポンジ ケーキでした！ そして クリスマスには どこへも 行きませんでした。あー つまらない クリスマス！！

でも、お正月は すばらしかったですよ！ おとしだまを たくさん もらいました。おとしだま というのは、お金で、きれいな 小さい ふうとうに はいっています。子どもは みんな お正月に おとしだまを もらいます。お父さんやお母さんや しんせきの 人から もらいます。

じゃ、今日は、これで...。お元気で。さようなら。

1月10日　　　ジョンより

PS. きのう、田中くんに クラスの しゃしんを とって もらいました。田中くんは 来週 しゃしんを くれるから つぎの 手紙で 一まい おくります。

わかりましたか

1 Using what you know about the verbs for giving and receiving, can you guess the meaning of the underlined phrases?

2 Can you say the following?

a I did not go anywhere.

b I did not receive anything.

c Nobody bought me a present.

3 Write a reply to John's letter, telling him about a celebration in your family.

31 Doing favours

Between other people

A does something for B.

A さん は	B さん に	verb て form	あげます

れい

れいこさんは トムくんに プレゼントをかってあげました。

Reiko bought Tom a present.

B receives assistance from A.

B さん は	A さん に	verb て form	もらいます

れい

トムくんは れいこさんに プレゼントをかって もらいました。

Tom had a present bought for him by Reiko. (Reiko bought Tom a present.)

Between the speaker and others who are equal or junior

The speaker includes members of the speaker's family and friends.

I/we do something for B.

(私 は)	B さん に	verb て form	あげます

れい

(私は) たろうくんに 本を かしてあげました。　　I lent a book to Taroo.

パーティーのじゅんび、てつだってあげるよ。　　I will help you prepare for the party.

I/we will get B to do something for me/us.

(私 は)	B さん に	verb て form	もらいます

れい

(私は) トムくんに 本を かしてもらいます。　　Tom will lend me the book

　　　　　　　　　　　　　　　　　　　　　　　　or I will get Tom to lend me the book.

兄に宿題をしてもらいます。　　　　　　　　　　I will get my brother to do my homework.

Note: 〜てもらいます is commonly used to express the idea that someone does something for me or us. In the future tense 〜てもらいます can imply persuasion (I will get him to do it for me). The following is also used.

B does something for me/us.

B さん は	verb て form	くれます

れい

トムくんが 本をかしてくれました。　　　　　Tom lent me a book.

お母さんが このドレスをつくってくれました。　Mum made me this dress.

Between the speaker and others who are senior to the speaker

Miss A kindly does something for me/us.

Senior person が Miss A	(私 に)	verb て form	くださいます

れい

先生が本を かしてくださいました。

The teacher kindly lent me a book.

先生のお父さんが ふるいしゃしんを見せてくださいました。

The teacher's father kindly showed us some old photos.

I/we received a favour from Miss A.

Miss A kindly does something for me/us.

(私は)	senior person に Miss A	verb て form	いただきます

れい

先生に 本をかしていただきました。

The teacher kindly lent me a book. (I received the kindness of a book loan from the teacher.)

すずきさんに おもしろい話をしていただきました。

Mr Suzuki kindly told us an interesting story.

Note: There is a little difference in meaning between the two ways of saying the same thing but note the difference in the particles.

You do not use ～てあげます when you speak to a senior person. It sounds rude. ～てさしあげます should also be avoided as it sounds patronising.

れい

先生: こくばんがきたないね。きれいにしなくちゃ。

せいと: ぼくがします。*not* してあげます *or* してさしあげます。

AB 63

Complete the pairs of sentences below with one of the following verbs. More than one answer is possible. Give the meaning of your sentence.

あげました、もらいました、くれました、くださいました、いただきました

1　よしおくんにいぬをあらって …
　　よしおくんがいぬをあらって …

2　お母さんにケーキをつくって …
　　お母さんがケーキをつくって …

3　おいしゃさんにうちへ来て …
　　おいしゃさんがうちへ来て …

4　女の人にみちをおしえて …
　　女の人がみちをおしえて …

5　先生にしゃしんを見せて …
　　先生がしゃしんを見せて …

6　弟に本をよんで …
　　弟が本をよんで …

十二支 (じゅうにし)

At New Year the name of the year changes according to the Chinese calendar. Twelve animals symbolise each year of a twelve-year period. People in Japan and China know under which animal sign they are born and in which they are now living. Few really believe it has any significance for their lives, but at New Year everyone reads their fortune for the year just for fun. Find your sign and read your fortune. Note: special kanji are used for the twelve animals.

ねずみ 子 — The rat

1960 1972 1984 1996

ゆうめいなねずみ年の人
ヒュー・グラント
キャメロン・ディアズ
アントニオ・バンデラス
ショーン・ペン

- りょこうが大好き
  ですね。
- ゴシップが好きで
  すね。
- クラシックな人で
  すね。
- やさしいですね。

今年は…
- トラブルはあまりあ
  りませんよ。
- デートでいそがし
  いですよ!
- 小さいロマンスも
  あります。

!いちばんいいともだち:たつ
!いちばんいいけっこんのあいて:うし、たつ、さる
!いちばんわるいけんかのあいて:うま

うし 丑 — The ox

1961 1973 1985 1997

ゆうめいなうし年の人
ジョージ・クルーニー
メグ・ライアン
ジム・キャリー
ケイト・モス

- とてもつよい人
  ですね。
- がんこです。
  (stubborn)
- しょうじきですね。
  (honest)
- あたまがいいですね。

今年は…
- ジレンマがおおい
  です。
- バリアをとりましょう。
- よくがんばります。
- あたらしいともだちが
  できます。

!いちばんいいともだち:いのしし
!いちばんいいけっこんのあいて:ねずみ、とり、へび
!いちばんわるいけんかのあいて:ひつじ

とら 寅 — The tiger

1962 1974 1986 1998

ゆうめいなとら年の人
トム・クルーズ
デミ・ムーア
レオナルド・ディカプリオ
エンヤ

- デリケートな人です。
- チャーミング
  ですね。
- エネルギーがあり
  ますね。
- よくおこりますね。

今年は…
- 海のレジャーがた
  のしいですよ。
- サーフィンもするで
  しょう。
- お金をもらうで
  しょう。
- 友だちができるで
  しょう。

!いちばんいいともだち:うま
!いちばんいいけっこんのあいて:いぬ、いのしし、うま
!いちばんわるいけんかのあいて:へび、さる

うさぎ 卯 — The rabbit

1963 1975 1987 1999

ゆうめいなうさぎ年の人
ブラッド・ピット
ニコラス・ケイジ
ヘレン・ハント
ジョン・クリース

- あかるい人ですね。
- はなしがじょうず
  です。
- よくけんかしますね。
- やさしくて、人気があ
  りますね。

今年は…
- にぎやかな年です。
- ロマンスがあります。
- べんきょうのペースは
  はやいですね。
- スポーツもやります
  ね。

!いちばんいいともだち:うさぎ
!いちばんいいけっこんのあいて:いぬ、いのしし、ひつじ
!いちばんわるいけんかのあいて:とり

たつ 辰　The dragon

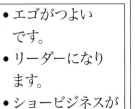

1964 1976 1988 2000

ゆうめいなたつ年の人
キアヌ・リーブズ
ロビン・ウィリアムズ
コートニー・コックス
ジョン・レノン

- エゴがつよい
です。
- リーダーになり
ます。
- ショービジネスが
好きですね。
- いいともだちがい
ます。

今年は…
- せいこうのチャン
スがありますよ。
- とてもラッキーな
年になります。
- でも、気をつけて!

!いちばんいいともだち:さる
!いちばんいいけっこんのあいて:とり、ねずみ、さる
!いちばんわるいけんかのあいて:いぬ

へび 巳　The snake

1965 1977 1989 2001

ゆうめいなへび年の人
ピアース・ブロスナン
チャーリー・シーン
オプラ・ウインフリー
ボブ・ディラン

- じょうねつてきです
ね。(passionate)
- きれい/ハンサム
です。
- お金のしんぱいは
ありませんね。

今年は…
- べんきょうはスロー
ダウンします。
- もっと、がんばっ
て!

!いちばんいいともだち:うさぎ
!いちばんいいけっこんのあいて:うし、とり、ねずみ
!いちばんわるいけんかのあいて:とら

うま 午　The horse

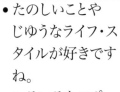

1966 1978 1990 2002

ゆうめいなうま年の人
サンドラ・ブロック
ジャッキー・チャン
シンディー・クロフォード
ハリソン・フォード

- たのしいことや
じゆうなライフ・ス
タイルが好きです
ね。
- いろいろなスポー
ツがとくいですね。

今年は…
- よくりょこうしてべ
んきょうもせいこう
するでしょう。
- スポーツも とても
じょうずになるでし
ょう。

!いちばんいいともだち:とり
!いちばんいいけっこんのあいて:とら
!いちばんわるいけんかのあいて:ひつじ、いぬ

ひつじ 未　The sheep

1967 1979 1991 2003

ゆうめいなひつじ年の人
ジュリア・ロバーツ
ビル・ゲイツ
メル・ギブソン
ブルース・ウィリス

- かしこい人ですね。
(wise)
- やさしくて、しんせ
つですね。
- おとなしい人です
ね。

今年は…
- ロマンスがあります。
- いろいろな人にあっ
てともだちになりま
す。
- せが高くなります。
- ラッキーな年です。

!いちばんいいともだち:いのしし、うま
!いちばんいいけっこんのあいて:うま
!いちばんわるいけんかのあいて:いぬ

さる 申　　　　　　　　　　The monkey

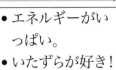

1968 1980 1992 2004

ゆうめいなさる年の人
ジリアン・アンダーソン
ウィル・スミス
ジェニファー・アニストン
トム・ハンクス

- エネルギーがいっぱい。
- いたずらが好き！
- あたまがいいですね。
- 人のまねがとてもじょうずですね。

今年は…
- とてもいそがしい！
- ユニークなプランがまっていますよ！
- あまりいそがないほうがいいですね。

!いちばんいいともだち:たつ
!いちばんいいけっこんのあいて:ねずみ
!いちばんわるいけんかのあいて:へび

とり 酉　　　　　　　　　　The rooster

1969 1981 1993 2005

ゆうめいなとり年の人
カイリー・ミノーグ
グロリア・エステファン
スティーブ・マーティン
ミシェル・ファイファー

- おもしろい人ですね。
- おしゃべりが好き！
- ちょっとかわっていて目立ちますね。
- エゴがつよいですね。

今年は…
- 気をつけて！
- 大きなものにチャレンジします。
- なきたい時もあります。
- よくはたらきます。

!いちばんいいともだち:たつ、うま
!いちばんいいけっこんのあいて:うし
!いちばんわるいけんかのあいて:ねずみ

いぬ 戌　　　　　　　　　　The dog

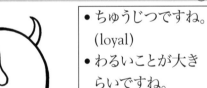

1970 1982 1994 2006

ゆうめいないぬ年の人
マドンナ
マイケル・ジャクソン
マライア・キャリー
エルビス・プレスリー

- ちゅうじつですね。(loyal)
- わるいことが大きらいですね。
- ちょっとうるさいです。

今年は…
- いそがしい年です。
- お金が入ります。
- ともだちがたくさんできます。
- いいニュース！

!いちばんいいともだち:とら
!いちばんいいけっこんのあいて:うさぎ
!いちばんわるいけんかのあいて:たつ

いのしし 亥　　　　　　　　The wild pig

1971 1983 1995 2007

ゆうめいないのしし年の人
ヴァル・キルマー
ミニー・ドライバー
ウィノナ・ライダー
エルトン・ジョン

- パーティーで人気がありますね。
- よくお金をつかいます。
- べんきょうとあそびにがんばりますね。

今年は…
- すばらしいことがありますよ！
- いいプランもあるでしょう。
- りょこうするでしょう。
- あまりいそがないで！

!いちばんいいともだち:いのしし
!いちばんいいけっこんのあいて:ひつじ
!いちばんわるいけんかのあいて:さる

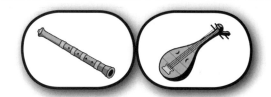

びわ: You are an exchange student in Japan shopping for presents for your family back home. You have found this amazing gift shop that has lots of interesting items. The shop keeper offers to help you choose suitable gifts. You have ¥10 000 to spend.

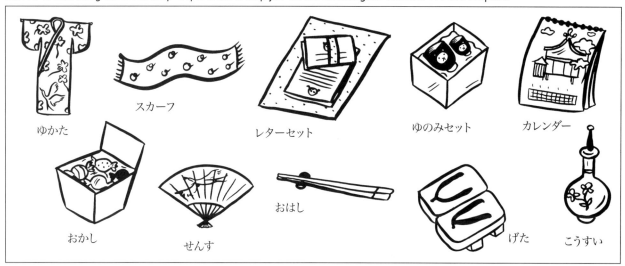

しゃくはち: You are a Japanese student working part-time at this souvenir shop. びわ is an exchange student from Australia shopping for presents for his/her family back home. Help びわ to choose presents. You may ask questions about his/her family in order to help びわ. Here is the price list:

ゆかた	¥3000	スカーフ	¥1400
レターセット	¥600	ゆのみセット	¥1200
おはし	¥300	げた	¥2300
日本のカレンダー	¥2000	せんす	¥1600
おかし	¥1000	こうすい	¥4500

れい

しゃくはち： いらっしゃいませ。何かおさがしですか。

びわ： ええ、家族におみやげをさがしています。父と母と姉と弟です。

しゃくはち： ええっと、お母さんにこうすいはいかがですか。

びわ： そうですね。母はこうすいが好きじゃないです。

しゃくはち： そうですか。ええっと、お母さんは何才ぐらいですか。

びわ： 40 才です。

しゃくはち： じゃあ、このスカーフはいかがですか。

びわ： ああ、きれいですね。いくらですか。

しゃくはち： 1400 円です。

びわ： ああ、そうですか。じゃあ、それにします。

チェックしましょう

クリスマスの買い物

あたたかい	warm
キャラクター	characters
〜こ	counter for small things
そんなに	so, such
ねだん	price
はながら (花がら)	flower pattern
わかい	young

日本のクリスマス

あけましておめでとう	New Year's greeting
おとしだま (お年だま)	gift of money at New Year
おめでとう	congratulations
かねもち (金もち)	rich person
かわいい	cute
おしょうがつ (お正月)	New Year
〜そう	looks like
ちょきん する	to save (money)
もらう ⑤	to receive

お正月

あさひ (朝日)	dawn, sunrise
えらい	great, amazing
(お) ぞうに	soup with omochi in it
だんだん	gradually
つく ⑤	to stick, adhere
どうした	what, what happened?
とりだす ⑤	to take out, remove
ねむる ⑤	to slumber, sleep
はつもうで	first visit to a shrine at New Year
ひどい	awful, cruel, rough
ベタベタ	sticky, tacky
(お) もち	rice cakes
やっぱり	still, I guess, as I thought

ジョンくんの手紙

くれる ⑤	to give (to me)
しんせき	relatives, relations
とうとう	in the end, finally
なにも … neg.	nothing, not anything
ふうとう	envelope

I can:
- shop for various items
- follow a store guide
- say how things appear
- understand informal speech
- express congratulations
- discuss giving and receiving items and favours
- read and write letters about celebrations
- follow a Chinese horoscope
- recognise and write the following kanji

正 早 買 週 朝 来 白

Unit 6

オーストラリアでの 休み
Holidays in Australia

オーストラリアのクリスマスホリデー

CD1
track 36–40

On their return to Japan four exchange students are interviewed by a reporter and the interview is published in the local newspaper. Find out what they thought of their experiences in Australia.

特集 オーストラリアのクリスマスホリデー

今日は、オーストラリアのホリデーについて、日本人りゅうがくせいに聞きたいと思います。

—お名前は。

かげやましょうこです。

—どのくらいオーストラリアにいましたか。

十月から一月まで三ヵ月いました。

—一番おもしろかったこと？

さあ、そうですねぇ。あ、クリスマスにキャンプに行きました。

—どんなことをしましたか。

一週間ぐらい、テントをもってビーチへ行きました。さかなつりをしたり、およいだり、サーフィンをならったりしました。とてもたのしかったです。

—クリスマスの日？

クリスマスの朝は、教会へ行きました。うちに帰って、ごちそうを食べました。大きいクリスマスツリーが居間にあって、その下にたくさんプレゼントがおいてありました。私もすてきなTシャツをもらいました。そしてその日はプールでおよいだり、テレビを見たりしました。

—日本のクリスマスとくらべてどうでしたか。

オーストラリアの方がたのしいと思います。

—どうもありがとう。

わかりましたか

Read the interview with Kageyama Shooko. In your notebook, indicate if the following statements are TRUE (T), FALSE (F), or NOT KNOWN (NK). Give reasons for F and NK answers.

1 Shooko was in Australia for one month.
2 The most interesting thing she did was go camping.
3 Shooko learned to surf.
4 The whole family went to church on Christmas morning.
5 Shooko gave everyone a T-shirt.
6 Shooko thinks that Christmas in Australia is more fun than Christmas in Japan.

—お名前は。
せんだとおるです。
—どのくらいオーストラリアにいましたか。
ぼくは十二月から二月まで三ヶ月です。
—どうでしたか。
ぼくのホストファミリーは中国人の家族でした。だから、えい語も中国語も教えてくれました。クリスマスは教会へ行きました。それから、レストランで食事をしました。一月一日は、何もしませんでしたが、かわりに二月十日にお祝いをしました。
—どんなことをしましたか。
しんせきの人や友だちが来てすごいごちそうを食べて、にわから花火を見ました。

—こんにちは。お名前は。
くぼひろしといいます。
—オーストラリアのクリスマスはどうでしたか。
ぼくはマイヤーさんという家族にお世話になりました。クリスマスはお祝いをしませんでしたが、そのかわりハナカというおまつりがあって、すごいディナーを食べました。そして、2週間ぐらい海へ行きました。ごうかなホリデーユニットにとまって、毎日朝からおよいだり、テニスをしたりして、すごしました。雨の日はビデオやコンピューターゲームをしてあそびました。
—よかったですねぇ。どうもありがとう。

わかりましたか

Find these expressions:

1 They taught me both English and Chinese.
2 instead we celebrated on February 10th.
3 … we did not do anything …
4 … we set off fire crackers.
5 Relatives and friends came over
6 … terrific feast …
7 I was looked after by a family called Myer.
8 Instead there was a festival called Hanukkah …
9 We stayed at a superb holiday unit …

日本のプディング

ちょっと…

クリスマスのごちそうはどう？

—お名前は。

のむらみさえといいます。

—あなたのクリスマスはどうでしたか。

クリスマスのごちそうを見て、びっくりしました。それはとっても大きいしちめんちょうのまるやきでした。デザートにはプディングとアイスクリームがありました。

—おいしそうですねえ。

ええ。とてもおいしいディナーでしたが、プディングはちょっと…。日本のクリスマスケーキのほうがおいしいと思いました。

—どうもありがとう。

私のホストファミリーには小さい子どもが四人いて、とてもかわいかったです。みんな大きいくつ下をぶらさげてサンタクロースを待っていました。お母さんは日本語の先生で、子どもたちもみんな日本語をならっていました。お母さんはとてもおいしいケーキやフルーツパイやビスケットを作ってくれました。

わかりましたか

1 In your notebook, indicate if the following sentences are TRUE (T) or FALSE (F). Give reasons for F answers.

  a みさえさんは ホストファミリーの 子どもが かわいいと 思っています。

  b The children hung up pillow cases.

  c Misae's host mother is learning Japanese.

  d Misae was very surprised by the turkey.

  e みさえさんは クリスマス・プディングが だい好きでした。

2 List the experiences that each student enjoyed with their families.

  a Shoko Kageyama

  b Tooru Senda

  c Hiroshi Kubo

  d Misae Nomura

3 Interview your friends about their holidays.

——こんにちは。お名前は？

さかぐちけんたといいます。

——オーストラリアはどうでしたか。

すごくよかったです。

11月と12月、2ヶ月間、アリさんという家族におせわになりました。アリさんの家族は イスラム教で、ラマダンという1ヶ月のだんじきをしていました。 そして、そのおわりに、おまつりがありました。

——どんなおまつりでしたか。

その日のあさ、家族みんなでモスクに行きました。ホストのお父さんはぼくもモスクにはいってもいいと言ってくれましたから、いっしょにはいりました。とてもきれいなモスクでした。おいのりのあと、友だちやしんせきの人にあいさつをしました。

——そのあとどんなことをしましたか。

うちにかえって、ホストのお母さんとお姉さんがすごいごちそうをつくってくれました。そして、しんせきの人や友だちが来て、ごちそうを食べたり、子どもたちにプレゼントをあげたりしました。ちょっと日本のお正月ににていると思いました。

わかりましたか

1 What was the highlight of Kenta's stay in Australia?

2 From the context guess the meaning of the following:

  a だんじき

  b おいのり

  c しんせきの人

  d あいさつをしました

  e にていると思いました

32 Asking for opinions

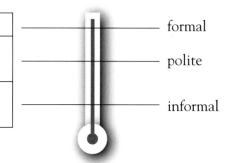

オーストラリアは	いかが ですか / でしたか
	どう ですか / でしたか
	どう 思いますか / 思いましたか
	どう? / だった?
	どう 思う? / 思った?

formal — polite — informal

How is/was Australia?

What do/did you think of Australia?

Note: いかが ですか and どう ですか are also used to offer something.

（れい）

コーヒーは いかが ですか / どう ですか。 　　　How about some coffee?

33 Giving opinions

AB 74, 77

(わたしは) opinion in plain form +	と	思います or 思っています	I think (that)
	と	思いました	I thought (that)

（れい）

1　The statement ends with noun or な adjective です.

田中さん		です。	It is Mr Tanaka.
田中さん	だ と 思います。		I think it is Mr Tanaka.
とても きれい		です。	It is very pretty.
とても きれい	だ と 思います。		I think it is very pretty.

Negative

田中さん じゃない		です。	It is not Mr Tanaka.
田中さん じゃない	と 思います。		I don't think it is Mr Tanaka.
あまり きれい じゃない		です。	It isn't very clean.
あまり きれい じゃない	と 思います。		I don't think it is very clean.

2　The statement ends with い adjective です.

| おもしろい | です。 | It is entertaining. |
| おもしろい | と 思います。 | I think it is entertaining. |

Negative

| 高くない | です。 | It isn't expensive. |
| 高くない | と 思います。 | I don't think it is expensive. |

3   The statement ends with a verb.

田中さんは あした また 来ます。   Tanaka will come again tomorrow.

田中さんは あした また ┌来る┐と 思います。   I think Tanaka will come again tomorrow.

Negative

田中さんは あした 来ません。   Tanaka won't come tomorrow.

田中さんは あした ┌来ない┐と 思います。   I don't think Tanaka will come tomorrow.

The tense of 思う and the opinion do not have to be the same.

冬はさむかったと 思います。   I think (now) the winter was cold.

冬はさむいと 思いました。   I thought (at the time) 'Winter is cold'.

Note: Japanese people avoid presuming to know what others are thinking except in general terms.
When stating what others think │〜と思っています│ is used.

（れい）

日本人は オーストラリアは きれいなくにだ と思っています。

イディオム

〜と思います is commonly used after たい.

（れい）

オーストラリアについて はなしたいと思います。   I'd like to talk about Australia.

It makes the statement sound less aggressive and therefore more polite than オーストラリアについて はなしたいです。

AB 78

1   Change the following statements into opinions using と思います.

    a 日本の いえの きそくは ふくざつです。

    b 幸子さんは ニュー・イヤーズ・イブのパーティーに 行きました。

    c オーストラリアの ステーキは 高くないです。

    d 今、さくらの花が とても きれいです。

    e 幸子さんは ちょっと はずかしかったです。

    f オーストラリア人は えらいです。

    g ジョンさんは おぞうにをたべました。

    h えみこさんは パーティーに 来ません。

2   Answer the following questions giving your opinion.

    a オーストラリアの夏はどう ですか。

    b 先週のテストはどうだった？

    c 日本のりょうりはどうですか。

    d フットボールは どう？

    e この学校のこうそくは きびしいと 思いますか。

    f 夏休みはよかったですか。

    g 日本へ行きたいですか。

Don't use と思います to make statements about your own actions. For example,
'I think I will go to Japan next year' can be expressed as 来年日本へ行きたいと思う
not 来年日本へ行くと思う.

In answer to a question such as 来年日本へ行きますか you can say はい、日本へ行くと
思います。

34 Making comparisons

Saying A is more 〜 than B

A のほうが (A は)	B より	adjective	です。

れい

東京のほうが よこはまより 大きいです。   Tokyo is bigger than Yokohama.

The word order can be the other way round:

B より	A のほうが	adjective	です。

れい

日本より中国のほうが大きいです。   China is bigger than Japan.

How is A compared to B?

(A は) B とくらべて

どうですか （でしたか）。 どう思いますか （思いましたか）。

れい

日本のお正月のおいわいはニュー・イヤーズ・イブとくらべてどう思いましたか。

What did you think of the celebration of Japan's Oshogatsu compared to New Year's Eve?

Asking which is more 〜 A or B

Which (do you think) is more 〜 A or B?

A と	B と	どっち (の ほう) が

〜〜ですか。or 〜〜と思いますか。

れい

サッカーと やきゅうと どっちのほうが おもしろいですか。

Which is more interesting, soccer or baseball?

たろうくんと じろうくんと どっちが せが高いと思いますか。

Who do you think is taller, Taroo or Jinoo?

Note: In written or formal language どちら is used rather than どっち.

Answering comparison questions

A is better/more delicious etc. or

I think A is more 〜.

A (の ほう) が

adjective

です。or と 思います。

れい

日本の お正月のおいわいのほうがたのしいと 思います。

I think that Japan's Oshogatsu celebration is more enjoyable.

サッカーがおもしろいです。

Soccer is more fun.

Accepting/rejecting food and drink

When you are asked:

コーヒーと こうちゃと どっちのほうが いいですか。　　Which do you prefer, coffee or tea?

you answer:

コーヒー（こうちゃ）をおねがいします。　　Coffee (tea) please.

or

コーヒー（こうちゃ）が いいです。(informal)

or

いいえ、けっこうです。　　　　　　　　　　Nothing, thank you.

---

1 Ask and answer questions about the following using くらべて.

> **れい**
> **Q:** このジーンズは あのジーンズとくらべて どう思いますか。
> **A:** あのジーンズのほうが 好きです。

a シドニー、ブリスベン
b パース、アデレード
c サッカー、ラグビー
d けんどう、すもう
e 中国のりょうり、日本のりょうり

2 Find out your friends' opinions of television programs using
AとBと どっち（のほう）が〜〜ですか。
or
AとBと どっち（のほう）が〜〜と思いますか。

3 Prepare questions for the following answers.

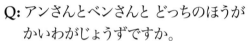

> **れい**
> **A:** アンさんのほうがじょうずだと 思います。
> **Q:** アンさんとベンさんと どっちのほうが かいわがじょうずですか。

a とうきょうのほうが にぎやかだと 思います。
b ピザのほうが おいしいと 思います。
c さっぽろのほうが さむいです。
d 日本の にわの ほうが きれいだと 思います。
e 花見のほうが たのしいと 思います。
f すもうのほうが おもしろいと 思います。
g すきやきのほうが おいしいと 思います。
h おふろのほうが 気もちがいいと 思います。

---

35 Asking what was the most 〜 thing

一番 いちばん	adjective	こと は or noun は	何ですか。

AB 71

> **れい**

一番たのしかったことは何ですか。	What was the most enjoyable thing?
五月に東京に行ったことです。	I went to Tokyo in May.
一番おもしろかったえいがは何ですか。	What was the most interesting film?
ハリー・ポッターです。	Harry Potter.

36 Stating that something is the most ～

(group word)	で (は) の中で (は)	subject が	一番 adjective (thing) です。

れい

日本の山 で (は) ふじ山 が 一番 高い (山) です。

Of the mountains in Japan, Mt Fuji is the highest.

クラスの中で (は) ケンさんが 一番 せが高いです。

Of the class members, Ken is the tallest.

Note: (Group) can be A と B と C では out of A, B and C.

れい

やきとりと すきやきと てんぷらでは すきやきが 一番 高いです。

Of yakitori, sukiyaki and tempura, sukiyaki is the most expensive.

The most ... one is/was ...

Group word で	一番 adjective	のは ことは	thing/event	です。

れい

日本のりょうりで 一番 おいしいのは すし です。

Of Japanese dishes, the most delicious one is sushi.

北海道のりょこうで 一番 おもしろかった ことは何ですか。スキーです。
(ほっかいどう)

Of your travel in Hokkaido, what was the most interesting thing? Skiing was.

せかいで 一番 ながい川はどの川ですか。ナイル川です。

Which is the longest river in the world? The Nile is.

このクラスで 一番せが高い人は だれ? ピーターさんです。

Who is the tallest person in this class? Peter is.

日本では 一番 にぎやかな ところは どこですか。東京です。

Which is the most bustling place in Japan? Tokyo is.

バーベキューで

1 Sachiko's host family have prepared a family barbecue. Listen to the conversation as the father prepares to cook the food.
2 What surprises Sachiko about the preparations?
3 Who eats first? Why?

CD1 track 41

クイズ

Can you answer ten questions? Listen to the radio quiz and enter the competition.

CD1 track 42

幸子さんの日本の家族への手紙

おじいさん、おばあさんへ

お元気ですか。
こちらは、まだまだ あつくて、週まつには 海へ行って およいでいますが、
日本では いかがですか。
私は 毎日 元気に オーストラリアの 生かつを 楽しんでいます。
ところで、今日は ほんとに びっくりしました。
"サプライズ・パーティー"を してくれたんです！
今日、3月8日は、私の17才の たんじょう日で、ちょうど 日曜日。
みんな、私のたんじょう日を わすれていると 思ったんですが、リビング・ルームへ
行って びっくり！ 大きな かみに "ハッピー・バースデー、さちこ!!"と
かいて、かべに はって ありました！
そして、ホスト・ファミリーが、みんなで「おたんじょう日、おめでとう！」と
言ってくれたんです。ほんとに うれしかった!!
プレゼントには 新しい Tシャツと サンダルを もらいました。
あとで、友だちが たくさん来て、カードとプレゼントをくれました。
みんなで いっしょに プールで およいで とても 楽しかったですよ。
それから、プールのそばで、にぎやかに お昼ごはんを 食べました。
今までで 一番 楽しい たんじょう日だったと 思います。
オーストラリアは、日本と くらべて、大きくて ひろいから、いえや にわも
大きくて、みんな パーティーや バーベキューをして 楽しんでいます。
私は オーストラリアは 本とうに いい くにだと 思います。
では、今日は これで、ペンを おきます。
お元気で。

　　　3月8日

　　　　　　　　　　　幸子より

わかりましたか

1 Give the meaning of the underlined sentences.

2 What does Sachiko say about Australia compared to Japan?

3 Sachiko's parents phoned to wish her a happy birthday.
Write the dialogue that took place.

イースターエッグって何？

Misae goes shopping with her host mother.

AB 73

わかりましたか

Find these expressions in the cartoon:

1 egg-shaped

2 symbol of new life

3 rabbits have lots of children

37 Answering the question 'why?'

The answer in plain form any tense	+ から (です)

れい

どうして パーティーに行きませんか。	Why aren't you going to the party?
びょうきだから(です。)	Because I am sick.
車がないから(です。)	Because I don't have a car.
せきがでるから(です。)	Because I have a cough.

漢字
かんじ

Kanji	Reading	Meaning		A way to remember
友	とも ユウ	friend		Two hands meeting as **friends** shake hands.
思	おも (う) おも (い) シ	to think, a thought, feeling		My 田 (paddy field) has a 心 (heart) under it, I **think**.
新	あたら (しい) シン	new		On the left a 木 (tree) with **new** growth on the top. On the right an 斤 (axe).
番	ばん (する) バン	to guard, number		ノ (katakana no) 米 (rice) over 田 (paddy field). Count the **number** of rice grains in the paddy field.
毎	マイ	every		人 (person) 母 (mother) **Every** person has a mother.
海	うみ カイ	sea		Water + every In the **sea** there is water everywhere.

Compounds

How many meanings can you guess? Write them out in your notebook.

友達	ともだち	一時間	いちじかん	思い出	おもいで
一年間	いちねんかん	新年	しんねん	一番	いちばん
毎日	まいにち	毎週	まいしゅう	海水	かいすい
毎年	まいとし/まいねん	毎朝	まいあさ	海外	かいがい

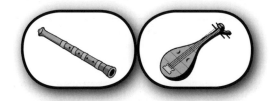

1 Discuss with your partner the members of your family and the members of his/her family. Make comparisons in regard to such things as height and opinions.

（れい）

A: 私の家族では、父が一番 せが高いです。

B: そう？ うちでは、母が一番 せが高いですよ！

A: へええ、そう？ お母さんのほうが、せが高い？

B: そうですよ！ でも、もうすぐ 兄のほうが 高くなると思います。

A: そうですか。お母さんも お兄さんも せが高いですね！

B: ところで、A さんの うちでは だれが 一番 よくテレビを 見ますか？

A: そうですねえ…やっぱり、妹が 一番 よく見ていると思いますね。

B: 妹さんは、どんな番ぐみが 一番 好きですか？

A: 妹は、おんがくやダンスが好きで、ヒットチャートの番ぐみを 見ています。

B: うちでは、兄も 私も コメディーが 一番 好きで よく見ますよ。

A: ドラマは どうですか。オーストラリアのドラマは アメリカのドラマとくらべて どう思いますか。

B: 私は、オーストラリアのドラマのほうが おもしろいと 思いますよ。でも、うちの父は アメリカ のドラマのほうが いいと言っています。

2 Talk about various things with your partner. Use any of the following topics.

a	(たべもの)	日本のたべもの	イタリアのたべもの	ちゅうごくのたべもの		
b	(おんがく)	ポップス	クラシック	カントリー・ウエスタン		
c	(スポーツ)	テニス	ラグビー	ネットボール	すいえい	スキー
d	(がいこく)	アフリカのくに	ヨーロッパのくに	アジアのくに	アメリカ	

You could begin your conversation on each of the topics like this:

（れい）

a オーストラリアの 食べものは、ちゅうごくの食べものと くらべてどう思いますか。

b どんな おんがくが 一番 好きですか。

c スポーツでは 何が 一番 とくいですか。

d ヨーロッパのくにと アジアのくにと どっちが 楽しいと思いますか。

チェックしましょう

オーストラリアでの休み

あいさつ	greeting
おいてある ⑤	is placed
(お) いのり	prayers
(お) いわいをする	to celebrate
おもう (思う) ⑤	to think
きょうかい (教会)	church
くつした (くつ下)	socks
くらべる ⑤	to compare
ごうか [な]	splendid, de luxe
ごちそう	feast, delicious food
しちめんちょう	a turkey
しょくじ (食事)	food, a meal
しんせき	relatives
そのかわり	instead
だんじきをする	to fast
にている ⑤	to resemble
ハナカ	Hanukkah, Jewish festival
はなび (花火)	fireworks
プディング	pudding
ぶらさげる ⑤	to hang up, suspend
(お) まつり	festival
まるやき	baked whole

イースターエッグって何?

いのち	life
かくす ⑤	to hide, conceal
かたち	shape
たまご	egg
ふっかつ	resurrection, revival
みつける	to find
(見つける) ⑤	

幸子さんの日本の家族への手紙

せいかつ (生かつ)	life, living

I can:

- discuss celebrations
- ask for and give opinions
- ask for and make comparisons
- accept and reject food and drink
- say which is the best …
- ask and answer why
- recognise and write the following kanji
  友　思　新　番　毎　海

よかと けんこう
Leisure and fitness

3

part

In these three units you will learn how to:
- talk about your leisure interests
- make comparisons
- talk about fitness and sport
- discuss music and movies.

You will also find out about clubs in Japan and the Kabuki theatre.

Contents

しゅみ
Hobbies

しゅみについてインタビュー

AB 85

CD2 track 1–5

Five high school students are asked about their leisure activities. Can you detect a reason for the enquiry?

B: まさあきくん

あなたはひまな時、どんなことをしますか。

ぼくは バンドをやっていて、たいてい バンドの れんしゅうをしています。

楽器（がっき）は 何を ひきますか。

ベースギターです。時々（ときどき） パーカッションもします。

そのバンドでは どんな 音楽（おんがく）をえんそうしますか。

うーん、ジャズや ロックがおおいです。

そうですか。ファミコンは どうですか。

時々友だちのうちでします。

どうして 友だちの うちで？

りょうしんが 「だめだ」 と 言うんです。

へぇー、きびしいですねぇ。どうも。

A: けんじくん

ひまな時、どんなことをするのが好きですか。

サッカーです。ぼくはクラブでサッカーをしていて、毎週（まいしゅう） 土曜日（どようび）の午後（ごご） しあいをします。

ほかのスポーツにもきょうみがありますか。

ええ。やきゅうも好きです。でも、やきゅうはするより見るほうが おもしろいですね。

じゃあ、うちにいるのと、外（そと）でスポーツをするのと、どっちのほうが 好きですか。

もちろん、外でスポーツをするほうがいいです。でも、雨（あめ）の日には 弟（おとうと）とファミコンをしたり、ゲームをしたりします。

わかりましたか

Match these expressions in the text above.

1 What kind of music do you perform?
2 What instruments do you play?
3 Wow, they are strict aren't they?
4 My parents say I'm not allowed.
5 Are you interested in other sports?

一番人気があるのはファミコン？

D: けい子さん

☆ あなたのしゅみは？

☆ いろいろあります…。

☆ ファミコンに きょうみが ありますか。

☆ いいえ、あんまり。クラリネットをふいたり、本を読んだりするのが好きです。でも 今は じゅけんでいそがしくて ぜんぜん ひまが ありません。

☆ へえ、じゅけん勉強は たいへんなんですねえ。

☆ ええ、じゅけんがはやく おわって、またクラリネットの れんしゅうをしたいと思います。クラリネットをれんしゅうするのが 一番好きなんです。

C: としえさん

☆ ひまな時、何をするのが 好きですか。

☆ 友だちと町へ行くのが 一番 好きです。町でえいがを見たり、買い物をしたりします。

☆ 買い物には どこへ行くのが 好きですか。

☆ はらじゅくや しぶやが 好きです。おもしろいみせが たくさん あるんです。

☆ ファミコンを するのが 好きですか。

☆ いいえ、あんまり…。うちにいるのは 好きじゃないんです。友だちと町へ行くほうが いいですね。

E: えみ子さん

☆ あなたは自由時間に何をしますか。

● ねるのが好きです。

☆ え？ ねるんですか？ ほかに好きなことはないんですか。たとえばファミコンとか…。

● ええ、大好きです。よる おそくまでファミコンを するから いつも ねむいんです。

☆ やっぱり ファミコンは おもしろいですね。

わかりましたか

1 How does each of the five spend their free time?

2 Match these expressions:

　a　I am very busy at the moment with exams.

b　That's hard, isn't it?

c　Are you interested in computer games?

d　Where do you like to go shopping?

38 Offering an explanation or justification

| Sentence 1 | Sentence 2 in plain form, all tenses |

+ の です。 ——— polite

ん です。 ———

の。 ——— informal

Sentence 2 ends with:

1 い adjective です。

れい

毎日およぎます。冬でもあたたかいん (の) です。

I swim every day. Even in winter it is warm, you see.

2 verb

れい

毎日 べんきょうしています。テストがあるん (の) です。

I am studying hard every day. There is a test, you see.

3 な adjective and noun

れい

かんじ カードをつくりました。かんじが にがてなん (の) です。

I made some kanji cards. I am weak at kanji, you see.

それは大きいはこですね。はい、がっきのはこなん (の) です。

That is a big box, isn't it? Yes, it's the instrument box, you see.

Note:

1 な is necessary after nouns or な adjectives, before ん or の です.

2 Sometimes ん (の) です is used to make the statement sound softer and there is little idea of giving an explanation or justification.

Connect a sentence on the left with a suitable sentence on the right and change it, adding ん (の) です.

1 今日、びょういんに 行きます。   a おもしろい みせがたくさんあります。

2 スポーツができませんでした。   b 電車が 来る。

3 はらじゅくへかいものに行きます。   c 雨が ふりました。

4 はしらなければならない。   d ほっかいどうは さむいですよ。

5 オーバーをわすれないでね。   e 母が びょうきです。

39 Talking about activities

Asking about likes—actions

| verb plain present | + のが | 好きですか。 | Do you like doing?

れい

およぐのが好きですか	Do you like swimming?
どんなことをするのが好きですか	What do you like doing?

Saying 'I like/don't like doing something'

| 私は | verb plain present | + のが
のは | 好きです。
好きじゃないんです。 |

Note: The particle changes to は in a negative sentence.

れい

本が好きです。	I like books.
本をよむのが好きです。	I like reading books.
テレビは好きじゃないんです。	I don't like TV.
テレビを見るのは 好きじゃないんです。	I don't like watching TV.

Saying that doing something is interesting/boring etc.

| Verb plain present | + のは | おもしろい です / つまらない です / etc. |

れい

えんそくに 行くのはたのしいです。	Going on an excursion is fun.
ここでおよぐ のは あぶないです。	Swimming here is dangerous.

Using the pictures and the following example dialogue, ask your classmates if they like doing these activities.

A: テレビを見るのが好きですか。

B: はい、大好きです。テレビを見るのは おもしろいです。

   or いいえ あんまり 好きじゃないです。テレビを見るのは つまらないんです。

Asking which of two things someone prefers doing

Verb 1 (dictionary)	のと	verb 2 (dictionary)	のと	どっちのほうが	いいですか。 or 好きですか。

れい

1   おはしで 食べる のと フォークで 食べる のと どっちのほうが いいですか。
      Which do you prefer—eating with chopsticks or with a fork?

2   えいがを見に行く のと うちでビデオを 見る のと どっちのほうが 好きですか。
      Which do you prefer—going out to see a movie or watching a video at home?

Answering 'Doing A is better' or 'I prefer doing A'

Verb dictionary form	ほうが	いい です or 好き です

れい

1   おはしで食べるほうが いいです。

2   うちで ビデオを 見るほうが 好きです。

Note: の does not come before ほうが in the answer.

Take turns to ask your partner which of two pairs of activities they prefer. Think up six pairs each.

イディオム

Expressions for playing music

〜を ひく (ひきます)	play stringed instruments, including piano
〜を ふく (ふきます)	play wind instruments
〜を する (します)	play percussion and general instruments
〜を やる (やります)	play in a band or orchestra
〜を えんそうする。(えんそう します)	give a performance, recital

〜あそぶ (あそびます) means play, relax, have fun in a general sense. It is not used for playing a sport or an instrument.

41 Stating preferences

Doing A is more … than doing B

A		B		
verb (dictionary form)	のは or ほうが	verb (dictionary form)	より	adjective です。

れい

かんじをよむのは or （ほうが）かんじをかくよりかんたんです。

Reading kanji is easier than writing kanji.

This is commonly said the other way around.

B	A		
verb (dictionary) より	verb (dictionary)	ほうが	adjective です。

れい

かんじをかくより、かんじをよむほうが かんたんです。

Than writing kanji, reading kanji is easier.

1 You have an exchange student visiting your family. How would you find out their preferences regarding the following?

  a Having a bath before dinner or after dinner.

  b Watching TV or listening to music.

  c Going to see a movie or going to watch football/netball.

  d Swimming in the sea or swimming in a pool.

  e Getting up early to go jogging with your father or sleeping in late.

2 State your own preferences in answer to the above questions.

3 Disagree with the following statements by stating the reverse.

  a ファミコンをするほうが、外で あそぶよりいいですね。

  b 朝はやくおきて、宿題をするより、よるするほうがいいですね。

  c 電話で友だちと話すより、E メールをかくほうがいいですね。

  d 一人で クラリネットをふくほうが、友だちとふくよりいいですね。

  e ポップスの音楽をきくより、クラシック音楽をきくほうがいいですね。

Listen to the radio interview of three elderly people. To what do they attribute their long, healthy lives?

ペンパルがほしい？

Read the advertisements for pen friends below. Choose the one you would like to correspond with. Give reasons for your choice. Write a reply.

山川かよ
1月20日生まれ
17才

私、バイクにのるのが大好きです。ひまな時は友だちとバイクで海に行ったり、山へ行ったりします。日本にはきれいなところがたくさんあるんですよ。いつか、バイクで日本中をりょこうしたいと思っています。りょこうが好きな人、バイクが好きな人、手紙をください。まっていまーす！
〒 102-0072
東京都千代田区一ツ橋 3-7-4

木本さおり
3月16日生まれ
16才

私はりょうりをするのが大好きです。とくに、おかしをつくるのが好きです。いろいろなくにのりょうりにきょうみがあります。りょうりが好きな人、ペンフレンドになってください。日本のいろいろなレシピをおくります。あなたのくにのレシピをおくってください。えいごでも、日本語でも OK です！
〒 590-0503
大阪市中央区大手通り 3-6-9

朝日金一
5月8日生まれ
18才

ぼくは、今、高校 3 年生。しけんがたくさんあって、毎日 7 時間ぐらい勉強しています。時々しゅうまつに、友だちとちかくの川へつりに行きます。それから、ぼくは 6 才からピアノをならっていて、クラシック音楽が好きです。ポップスは、あまり好きじゃないです。ぜひペンパルがほしいです。お手紙まっています。
〒 399-0025
長野県飯田市立山 1005

石口しんご
9月3日生まれ
16才

ぼくは、サッカーが大好きです。サッカークラブでおそくまでれんしゅうしたり、毎日 10 キロぐらいはしったり、しゅうまつもジムに行ってトレーニングしたり、とてもいそがしいです。でも、プロのサッカーせんしゅになりたいからがんばっています。ほかのしゅみは、スポーツの映画を見ることです。でも、スポーツは見るよりする方がおもしろいですね。
〒 631-0011
奈良市西登美丘 6 丁目 17-9

漢字
かんじ

Kanji	Reading	Meaning		A way to remember
音	おと オン	noise, sound		立 (たつ) to stand. If you stand on the sun you will make a **noise**.
楽	たの (しい) たの (しむ) ガク ラク	enjoyable, to enjoy, music, ease		A drum on a wooden stand, decorated with tassels for an **enjoyable time**.
午	ゴ	noon		A sundial shows us that it is **noon**.
後	あと うし (ろ) ゴ	after, rear, behind, later		Part of 行 (go) tells us one reading! The top part of 冬 (winter) comes **after** 彳.
物	もの ブツ モツ	thing		牛 (a cow) + a hairy tail—what a strange **thing**.
読	よ (む) トク ドク	to read		To say 言 plus to sell 売 is selling by saying, as in advertisements that we **read**.
勉	ベン	to exert oneself		The thing that is tied up, 免, uses strength 力, to **exert itself**.
強	つよ (い) キョウ ゴウ	strong		a 弓 (bow) katakana ム and 虫 (an insect). With my bow I'm **strong** enough to kill this giant insect!

Compounds

How many meanings can you guess?

音楽	おんがく	午前	ごぜん	午後	ごご
買い物	かいもの	食べ物	たべもの	強大	きょうだい
読書	どくしょ	読み物	よみもの	勉強	べんきょう

あきらくんからの E メール

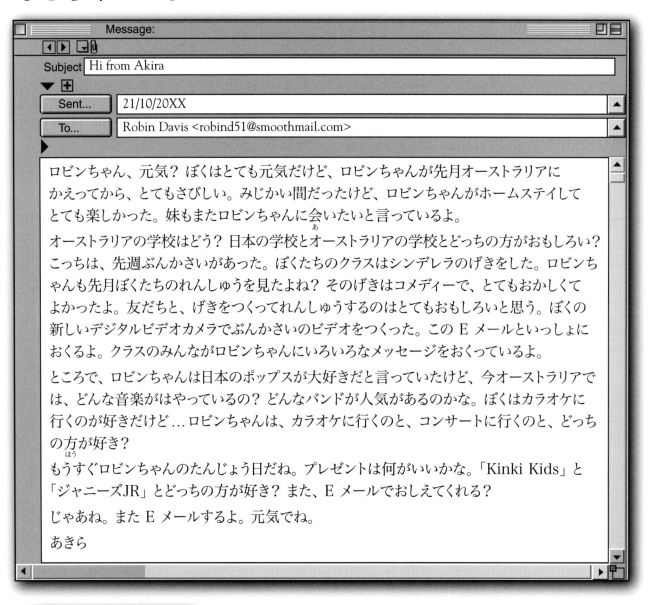

Message:		
Subject	Hi from Akira	
Sent...	21/10/20XX	
To...	Robin Davis <robind51@smoothmail.com>	

ロビンちゃん、元気? ぼくはとても元気だけど、ロビンちゃんが先月オーストラリアに
かえってから、とてもさびしい。みじかい間だったけど、ロビンちゃんがホームステイして
とても楽しかった。妹もまたロビンちゃんに会いたいと言っているよ。

オーストラリアの学校はどう? 日本の学校とオーストラリアの学校とどっちの方がおもしろい?
こっちは、先週ぶんかさいがあった。ぼくたちのクラスはシンデレラのげきをした。ロビンち
ゃんも先月ぼくたちのれんしゅうを見たよね? そのげきはコメディーで、とてもおかしくて
よかったよ。友だちと、げきをつくってれんしゅうするのはとてもおもしろいと思う。ぼくの
新しいデジタルビデオカメラでぶんかさいのビデオをつくった。この E メールといっしょに
おくるよ。クラスのみんながロビンちゃんにいろいろなメッセージをおくっているよ。

ところで、ロビンちゃんは日本のポップスが大好きだと言っていたけど、今オーストラリアで
は、どんな音楽がはやっているの? どんなバンドが人気があるのかな。ぼくはカラオケに
行くのが好きだけど…ロビンちゃんは、カラオケに行くのと、コンサートに行くのと、どっち
の方が好き?

もうすぐロビンちゃんのたんじょう日だね。プレゼントは何がいいかな。「Kinki Kids」と
「ジャニーズJR」とどっちの方が好き? また、E メールでおしえてくれる?

じゃあね。また E メールするよ。元気でね。

あきら

わかりましたか

1 In your notebook, indicate if the following statements are True (T), False (F) or Not Known (NK). For any statements that you mark as F, give reasons for your choice.

a Akira and Robin have never met in person before.

b Akira's sister wants to meet Robin.

c Akira's class put on a comedy version of Cinderella.

d Akira thinks practising sport is more fun than putting on a play.

2 What attachment does this email have?

3 What questions does Akira ask?

4 Guess what Kinki Kids and ジャニーズ JR are.

ジョンくん、クラブにはいらない？

AB 86

わかりましたか

In your notebook, indicate if the following statements are True (T), False (F) or Not Known (NK). For any statements that you mark as F, give reasons for your choice.

1 John's friend says that he isn't interested in Japanese sport.
2 John and his friend will meet at the gym tomorrow.
3 どうぐ means helmet.
4 まってる is a contraction of まっている.

5 The girl thinks John looks silly.
6 The word for kendo stick is しない.
7 こういうふうに means 'this way'.

Unit 7 : しゅみ Hobbies

115

わかりましたか

Can you find these expressions in the cartoon above?

1   You are awful.
2   Ouch!
3   I didn't mean to.
4   I don't think it suits me.
5   Japanese culture
6   I am interested
7   I wonder if it will be easier (more comfortable) than kendo.

わかりましたか

Can you find these expressions?

1 What is さどうぶ?
2 It is bitter.
3 Help!
4 My legs are numb. Like being dead.
5 What happened? An accident?

Note: ほうかご is the expression used for 'after school' rather than 学校のあとで.

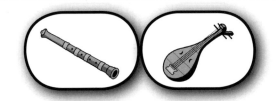

Take turns to be the interviewer. The one who is interviewed does not look at the book. Find out the personality of your partner by administering the following test.

Find out your partner's preferences by asking questions.

れい

1　一人で<u>勉強するの</u>と、友達と<u>勉強するの</u>と、どちらが好きですか。

Afterwards, count up the A and B answers and tell your partner whether they have type A, type B or type C personality!

しつもん		しつもん	
1　一人で勉強する	(A)	6　ウォークマンで音楽をきく	(A)
友達と勉強する	(B)	ロックコンサートに行って 　　音楽をきく	(B)
2　スポーツをやる	(A)	7　電話で友達と話す	(A)
スポーツを見る	(B)	コーヒーショップで友達と話す	(B)
3　山であそぶ	(A)	8　ファミリーレストランで食べる	(B)
海であそぶ	(B)	小さいレストランで食べる	(A)
4　ファミコンをする	(A)	9　友達と家族にプレゼントを 　　買ってあげる	(A)
トランプをする	(B)	友達と家族にプレゼントをもらう	(B)
5　ジーンズとTシャツをきる	(A)	10　小さいみせでいろいろ買う	(A)
スーツをきる	(B)	スーパーマーケットでいろいろ買う	(B)

タイプ A

こたえ－おもに A

あなたはきっと人より
どうぶつが好きでしょう。
しずかな人で一人で勉強する
のが好きです。
すくないけれど いい友達が
いますね。

タイプ B

こたえ－おもに B

あなたは人が
大好きですね。
元気でにぎやかな人ですね。
友達がたくさん
いますね。

タイプ C

こたえは－半分 A, 半分 B

あなたは時々一人で
勉強するほうが好きです。
でも、にぎやかなところが
しずかなところより好きですね。
早く友達ができますね。

チェックしましょう

しゅみについてインタビュー

えんそう する	to perform
がっき (楽器)	musical instrument
きょうみ	interest
きょうみがある ⑤	to have an interest
じゆうじかん(自由時間)	free time
たとえば	for example
にんき(人気) がある ⑤	be popular, be in vogue
ひく ⑤	to play a stringed instrument or piano
ファミコン	computer games
ほかの〜	other …
ほかに	besides
もちろん	of course
りょうしん	parents

ペンパルがほしい!

(お) かし	confectionery, cake
クラシック おんがく(音楽)	classical music
せんしゅ	player, athlete
はしる ⑤	to run
りょこう	travel

あきらくんからの E メール

おかしい	funny
げき	play, drama
シンデレラ	Cinderella
デジタルビデオカメラ	digital video camera
はやる ⑤	to be in fashion
ぶんかさい	cultural festival

ジョンくん、クラブにはいらない?

あう ⑤	to suit
けんどうぶ	kendo club
こういうふうに	in this way
しない	kendo fencing stick
たいいくかん	gymnasium
ほうかご	after school
めん!	kendo call
らく[な]	comfortable, easy

I can:

- talk about leisure time
- ask and say what I and others like doing
- say that doing something is interesting/boring
- ask and talk about preferences
- write a pen friend an email describing my interests
- recognise and write the following kanji
  音 楽 勉 強 午 後 物 読

スポーツとけんこう
Sports and fitness

CD2 track 11-16

リーダーズからの手紙

ファミコンの
やりすぎはきけん！
コンピューターは目に悪い。

高校生の60%は
スポーツをしない？
（今年の生活ちょうさより）

～小学校教師のシンポジウムで～
さいきんの 子どもは
うんどうがきらい！？

大きい町の子供達はなまけもの！

わかりましたか

The headlines above resulted in a storm of protest letters to the editor. What do the headlines and letters tell you about the lifestyles of young Japanese?

AB 97

こうえんがない
大阪市　主婦
三十二才

　私は　小学2年生と3年生の子どもがいますが、うちのちかくにこうえんがありません。学校のグラウンドもほうかごや日曜日はつかうことができません。かんとくの先生がすくないからです。うちの子どもはうんどうがきらいじゃないんです。やきゅうやラグビーが大好きです。でもグラウンドやこうえんがないんです。

あそぶ時間がほしい
中学二年生
男子K・T

　ぼくの学校では、じゅぎょうとじゅぎょうの間に、休み時間が十分あります。そのみじかい時間に、サッカーやハンドボールをれんしゅうしています。
　ほうかごもあそびたいけれどみんなできょうしつをそうじしなければなりません。それにみんなじゅくに行ったり、しゅうじやそろばんをならったりしているから、とてもいそがしいんです。もっとあそぶ時間がほしいです。

私はとてもけんこうです

高崎市　中学2年

女子Ｎ・Ｊ

私は　通学に一時間半かかります。

うちからえきまで自転車で十五分。電車にのって四十分。

そして　また　学校まで二十分あるかなければなりません。

新聞には「さいきんの子どもはうんどうをしない」とかいてありましたが、そうじゃないと思います。スポーツをする時間がないんです。でも私は一週間に三時間　自転車にのって、四時間あるいていて、とてもけんこうです。

なまけものといわないで！

高校2年

女子Ｓ・Ｉ

私はクラブはコーラスぶで、れんしゅうは火・木で　五時までです。月・水・金はじゅくに行きます。じゅくは五時半から八時半までです。毎日宿題もたくさんあるから、よる一時ごろまで勉強しなければなりません。日曜日はとてもつかれていて、何もしたくないです。朝は　おそくおきて　時々ファミコンであそびます。私はなまけていませんが、いそがしすぎて、スポーツをすることができないんです。ファミコンが一番リラックスできるんです。

どこでスポーツできますか

高校一年生

男子Ｈ・Ｍ

ぼくは　東京に住んでいます。うちのちかくのテニスコートは一か月前によやくしなければなりません。そして、コート代は一時間一万円です。とても高くて、ぼく達はびっくりしました。ぼく達はスポーツがしたいけれど、テニスコートもバスケットコートもありません。新聞に「高校生はスポーツをしない」という記事がありましたが、どこでできますか。

イディオム

Contractions are often used in writing. Find the contractions for the following.

1 月曜日
2 水曜日
3 金曜日
4 女の子
5 男の子

わかりましたか

What is the main point made in each letter?

42 Saying something is too much `AB` 98,104

やります +	すぎます →	やりすぎます。	do too much.
ちいさい +	すぎます →	ちいさすぎます。	too small.
にぎやか +	すぎます →	にぎやかすぎます。	too noisy

れい

くだものを 食べすぎて おなかがいたいです。

I ate too much fruit and my stomach hurts.

これは買いません。高すぎるんです。

I am not buying this, it is too expensive.

しずかすぎますね。けんちゃんは何をしていますか。

It is too quiet, isn't it? What is little Ken doing?

Note: すぎる ② is a verb which means 'to go past', 'to exceed'. すぎ attached to the stem of a verb creates a noun. For example やりすぎ means 'doing too much'.

Respond to the following situations using … すぎる

1 Your friend wants to visit you at 6 am. (はやい)

2 You try on a sweater and it is far too big. (大きい)

3 There is a good movie on TV. It starts at 11.30 pm and you have to be up early. (おそい)

4 Someone has put six spoonfuls of sugar in your coffee. (あまい)

5 Your legs hurt. You have been practising sport. (れんしゅうする)

6 Someone wants you to help them next week. You already have a full program. (いそがしい)

7 The neighbour's dog is leaping all over you. (元気)

43 How to say the time to do something or the time of doing something `AB` 95

Verb plain present	時間 (じかん)

れい

あそぶ時間はありません。

We don't have time to play.

つく時間をおしえてください。

Please let me know your time of arrival.

1 Ask your partner for information about the following times.

(れい)

School starts

学校がはじまる時間をおしえてください。

(use particle が)

a Bank opens (あく).

b Train leaves.

c Plane arrives.

d Movies finish.

e We board the ship.

2 Complete the sentences using the clues.

(れい)

Time to play

いそがしくて あそぶ
時間はありません。

a Time to sleep.

b Time to watch.

c Time to go out (でかける).

d Time to talk with friends.

e Time to read comic books.

44 Possible or not possible—can/can't do

AB 103

Noun	が できます
Verb (dictionary) こと	が できます

(れい)

日本語が できますか。	Can you speak Japanese?
はい、すこし できます。	Yes, I can a little.
この川で、およぐことが できますか。	Can we swim in this river?
はい、できます。or いいえ、できません。	Yes we can, *or* No we cannot.
その町で ゴルフをすることが できますか。	Can you play golf in that town?
はい、ゆうめいなコースが あります。	Yes, there is a famous course there.

Yukiko is deciding which school to attend while in Australia. What can she do at school A and school B?

Make a list following the example sentences.

(れい)

インターネットをつかうことができます。
コンピュータのへやがありますから。
or コンピュータのへやがあるんです。

Note: the spelling of 'computer' can be either コンピュータ, or コンピューター.

School A

コンピュータのへや	Computer room
プール	Swimming pool
テニスコート	Tennis courts
としょかん	Library
えんそく	School camp
ドイツ語のきょうしつ	German room
こうどう/ホール	Hall
おんがくしつ	Music room

School B

せいぶつしつ	Biology labs
ESL のきょうしつ	ESL room
たいいくかん	Gymnasium
ちょうりしつ	Home economics room
りかしつ	Science lab
グラウンド	Athletics ground
バスケットのコート	Basketball courts
日本語のきょうしつ	Japanese room

たんご

うけつけ	reception
かぜをひく	catch a cold
気分がわるい	feel unwell
ちゅうしゃする	give injection
げり	diarrhoea
ねつがある	have a fever
はきけがする	feel nauseous
はなみずがでる	have a runny nose
びょういん	hospital, clinic, surgery

わかりましたか

Listen to the conversation as you read the text above.

1　What is the doctor's first diagnosis?

2　What does she decide is wrong with John?

3　How does she treat this illness?

まことくんがけがをした！？

わかりましたか

Listen to the conversation as you read the text, then answer the following questions. Give reasons for your answers.

1　Why did John ring Makoto?

2　What happened to Makoto?

3　What impression do you have of Makoto?

45 Reported information

They say that …, it seems that …, apparently …

Sentence in plain form (all tenses)	+ そうです or そうだ

（れい）

まことくんはけがをしたそうです。

Apparently Makoto was injured.

今年の冬はさむいそうです。

They say it will be cold this year.

ジョンさん、日本へ行くそうですね。

I hear you are going to Japan, John. Is that right?

新聞によると、日本人はステーキが好きだそうです。

According to the paper, Japanese people like eating steak. (it seems)

Note: If the source of information is known to you or is from the media, you can say
〜によると (according to …).

（れい）

天気よほうによると、あしたは雪がふるそうです。

According to the forecast, it will snow tomorrow.

〜によると sounds too formal for casual conversation.

---

1 Change the following statements to mean 'According to the newspaper, it seems that …'
  a さいきんの子どもたちは うんどうが きらいです。
  b さいきんの中学生は ねるのが 好きです。
  c 高校の 2 年生は いそがしすぎます。
  d 中学生は よるおそくまで ファミコンをするから いつも ねむいです。
  e 大きい町のテニスコートは 1 か月前に よやくしなければなりません。

2 Share some information you have heard recently, using そうです.

まことくんはだいじょうぶ？

CD2
track 19

Listen to the conversation between John and Erika. Write answers to the following questions in your notebook.

1 What does John say has happened to Makoto?
2 What does Erika suggest that John does to please Makoto?
3 What does John agree to do?
4 What will Erika do?

漢字
かんじ

Kanji	Reading	Meaning		A way to remember
自	ジ	self		Put your finger on your nose, nose to indicate your **self**.
分	わ (かる) わ (ける) フン、プン ブン	to understand, to divide, minute, part		Use 刀 a sword to **divide** into 八 eight **parts** so that you can **understand**.
聞	き (く) き (こえる) ブン	to listen, to enquire, to be heard		耳 an ear at the 門 gate can **hear**.
活	カツ	living, energy		Water 氵 on the 舌 tongue is needed for **living**.
方	かた ホウ	way, manner		Point a torch this way to show the **direction**.
通	とお (る) とお (り) かよ (う) ツウ	to pass along, the street, to go to and from		マ Ma watches a caterpillar **passing along** in front of the security gate.

Compounds

How many meanings can you guess?

自分	じぶん	自転車	じてんしゃ	時分	じぶん
五分	ごふん	十分	じゅっぷん	新聞	しんぶん
生活	せいかつ	活気	かっき	通学	つうがく
通行	つうこう	文通	ぶんつう	交通	こうつう

漢字
かんじ

Kanji	Reading	Meaning	A way to remember
体	からだ タイ	body	a person 人 ... イ plus 本 foundation, a tree 木 with roots.
達	たっ (する) ダチ タチ	to reach, attain, plural ending	土 the earth is piled up over 羊 a sheep, who is afraid that the giant caterpillar will be able to **reach** him.
住	す (む) ジュウ	to live dwelling	人 a person is a small 王 king inside the dwelling where he **lives**.
事	こと ゴト	thing, action, fact	一口 one mouth and a broom linked together with a pole. A very strange **thing**, that's a **fact**.
々		A symbol used to repeat the preceding kanji, indicating a number of objects.	

Compounds

How many meanings can you guess? Write them out in your notebook.

住人	じゅうにん	住所	じゅうしょ	大事	だいじ
仕事	しごと	時々	ときどき	人々	ひとびと
山々	やまやま	体中	からだじゅう	体育	たいいく
私達	わたしたち	子供達	こどもたち	達人	たつじん

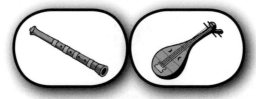

毎日新聞の
ライフスタイルチェック！

Ask your partner the following questions. Record their answers and add up the points (see page 130). Read out the appropriate advice. Swap roles.

1 しゅうまつは：

  a おそくまで ねていますか。
  b はやくおきて、ジョギングしますか。
  c 時々スポーツをしますか。

2 100m を：

  a 1分半ぐらいで、およぐことができますか。
  b はやくないけれど、およぐことができますか。
  c およぐことができませんか。

3 うんどうかいで：

  a いつも メダルを もらいますか。
  b スタンドで 食べたり、のんだり していますか。
  c とくいじゃないけれど、さんかしますか。(participate)

4 クロスカントリーは：

  a 好きじゃないから、さんかしませんか。
  b さいごまで (to the end) はしりますか。
  c あるいたり、はしったり しますか。

5 どれが 一番 好きですか。

  a ボーリング、スケート、ダンス
  b テニス、じょうば、エアロビクス
  c ラグビー、サッカー、すもう、バスケットボール

てんすう

Q	A	B	C
1	1	4	2
2	5	3	1
3	5	0	3
4	1	4	3
5	2	3	5

20–23

あなたは 本とうの スポーツマン / スポーツウーマンです。オリンピックを めざして (aiming for) がんばってください。そして、ひまな時は スポーツコーチになって、子どもたちにスポーツの楽しさをおしえて下さい。コーチをしたくない? じゃ、ロッククライミングか ウェイトリフティングはどうですか。

11–19

あなたは マイペースで がんばる タイプです。とても 元気で スタミナもあります。そのちょうしで 好きなスポーツを つづけてください。とても けんこうだから、スキューバダイビングや 水上スキーにチャレンジしてみて下さい。バンジージャンプもいいですよ。

5–10

あなたは スポーツがきらいで、ちょっと なまけものですね。もうすこし 体を つかわないと いけません。ダンスはどうですか。それから、毎朝 30 分ぐらい あるくほうがいいです。ヨガも 体に いいです。

チェックしましょう

リーダーズからの手紙

うんどう	exercise, movement
かんとく する	supervision, to supervise
きけん	danger, risk
きじ (記事)	news item, report
けんこう [な]	health(y)
コーラスぶ	choral society
さいきん	recently, lately
さいきんの	recent, latest
しゅうじ	calligraphy
じゅく	cram school
せいかつ (生活)	life, living
そろばん	abacus
ちょうさ	inquiry, investigation
つうがく する (通学する)	to attend school
なまけもの	a lazy person
よやく する	to book, reserve

まことくんがけがをした！？

おととい	the day before yesterday
おだいじに(お大事に)	look after yourself
かた	shoulder
かんごふ (さん)	nurse
からだ(体)	body
からだじゅう(体中)	all over the body
くび	neck
けがをする	be injured
さらいしゅう(さ来週)	the week after next
スノーボード	snowboarding
ちがでる	bleed
ほねをおる	break a bone

あなたの生活はどう？

うんどうかい	sports day
さいご	the last, the end
さんか する	to participate
ちょうし	form, condition, tune
てんすう	score, points
つづける ⓡ	to continue
マイペース	one's own pace
めざす ⓤ	to aim at, to have an eye on

I can:

- talk and read about healthy lifestyle
- explain simple health problems
- follow a health questionnaire
- say and understand 'do something too much'
- say and understand 'possible/not possible'
- say and understand reported information
- read and write the following kanji

  自 分 聞 活 通 方
  体 事 達 住 々

エンターテインメント
Entertainment

トップ 10

S.T.O.P.
ウイークリー・ミュージック・インフォメーション

全日本チャート トップ 10
ぜんにほん

1	夏まつり	ホワイトベリー
2	さよならバス	ゆず (YUZU)
3	雨のメロディー	キンキ キッズ (Kinki Kids)
4	好きだよ	モーニングむすめ
5	さよなら 大好きな人	花*花
6	ファーストラブ	うただひかる
7	セイ・マイ・ネーム	デスティニーチャイルド
8	YMCA	ビレッジピープル
9	オール・アイ・ハブ	バックストリートボーイズ
10	レット・イット・ビー	ビートルズ

CD2
track 21

ニュース フラッシュ
エルビス 生きてる!!??

AB 110(1)

ゴールド・コーストのムービー・ワールドで 3 人の高校生がエルビスを見たそうだ!!! ハンバーガーとチップスを食べて コーラを飲んでいたそうだ!!!

でも、サングラスをかけていたから、かおをよく見ることが できなかった! ざんねん! 三人の高校生は、あれはたぶん エルビスだろうと言っていた。ほんとうか? うそか?

食べ方、飲み方、あるき方は、エルビスと同じ！！せも
エルビスと同じぐらいだった! きっと、エルビスだ! エルビスは 生きている!

わかりましたか

1 Which of the top 10 are still popular?
2 List the ways in which this person resembled Elvis.

46 How to say how to do something or the way someone does something

verb ます	かた

かき　　かた

how to write/way of writing

れい

このかんじのかき方をおしえて下さい。

Please teach me how to write this kanji.

ドンさんのかき方はへんですね。

Don's way of writing is strange, isn't it?

AB 107

Choose a suitable ending from list B for the sentences in list A. Write out the sentences in your notebooks.

A
1　このゲームのやり方を
2　あの先生の話し方は
3　そのすわり方は
4　先生、このもんだいのやり方を
5　お母さん、このケーキのつくり方は

B
a　ぎょうぎがわるいです。
b　おしえてくれない？
c　何ページ？
d　はやくてよくわかりません。
e　おしえて くださいませんか。

47 Saying things are the same

AB 114(2)

A と	B は
A は	B と

同じです。
おな

A and B are the same.

A is the same as B.

If two things are approximately the same, say 同じぐらいです。

Talk about the following rock stars, using the example as a guide.

れい

A と B はヘアスタイルが同じです。

A　　　　　B　　　　　C　　　　　D

映画に行きませんか

CD2 track 22

1 もしもし、あのう、ジョンともうしますが、年子さんはいらっしゃいますか。

2 はい、はい。ちょっとまってください。年子、ジョンくんから電話だよ！

3 はーい。もしもし、ジョンくん、こんにちは。

4 こんにちは。年子さん、来週の日曜日、いそがしいですか。

5 来週の日曜日、ひまだと思いますけど…

6 じゃ、映画に行きませんか。

7 いいですねえ。行きましょう。何を見ましょうか。

8 「ハリーポッター」という映画を見ましたか。おもしろいそうですよ。

9 ああ、それはもう見たんです。ごめんなさい、ジョンくん。「ロードオブザリング」という話を読んだことがありますか。

11 その映画があるんですけど、見たいですか。

10 ええ、ありますよ。学校で読みました。

13 じゃあ、新しい 007 の映画はどうですか。

12 ぼくは、ファンタジーより アクションの方が好きなんです。

14 いいですね。じゃあ、日曜日、七時に前と同じところでまっています。

15 はい、七時ですね。

16 じゃ、おやすみなさい。

わかりましたか

1 二人はどの映画をえらびましたか。

2 ジョンくんはどんな映画が好きですか。

3 どうして「ハリーポッター」という映画を見に行きませんでしたか。

4 二人はどこであいますか。

48 Asking/telling about past experience

verb た form +	ことがあります (か)

AB 109, 115(2)

れい

アメリカへ 行った ことがありますか。	Have you been to America?
Answering:	
はい、あります。	Yes, I have.
いいえ、ありません。	No, I haven't.
ぼくもアメリカへ 行った ことがあります。	I have also been to America.

---

1 Ask your partner if he or she has ever done the following.

2 Make a list of your favourite books, films and songs. Find out how many of your classmates have read, seen or heard them.

れい

A: 〜〜という本をよんだことがありますか。

B: いいえ、ありません。おもしろいですか。

A: はい、とてもおもしろいです。おすすめします。

A: 〜〜という映画 を見たことがありますか。

B: はい、あります。きょ年見ました。かなしい映画ですね。

It is not apropriate to use 〜ことがあります for talking about a movie or novel that
has just appeared. It sounds as strange as it does in English to say 'have you ever seen'
or 'have you ever read' about a current movie or book.

ハリー・ポッターと
賢者の石
けんじゃ いし

あらすじ

ハリーは 11 才の誕生日にホグワーツまほう学
校から手紙をもらった。ハリーはふつうの男の
子と同じだったが、ほんとうはまほう使いだっ
た！ロンとハーマイオニーという新しい友達と
ホグワーツ学校での生活がはじまった。まほう
の世界には、ハリーのしらないふしぎな事がた
くさんあった。手紙をはこぶ ふくろうや、
クィディッチというまほう使いのスポーツ。それ
から、賢者の石のまほう使いのヴォルデモート
…ハリーはヴォルデモートの手から賢者の石
をまもる。

おすすめします AB 116

世界中でこの本はたくさんうれました。本を読
んだ後にこの映画を見ると、もっとおもしろい
と思います。映画では、SFX のえいぞうを楽
しむことができるでしょう。

わかりましたか

Select the correct statement from the following.

1 まほう means:
   a art
   b mystery
   c magic
   d music.

2 ふつうの男の子 means:
   a special boy
   b normal boy
   c cool boy
   d happy boy.

3 生活がはじまった means:
   a life started
   b adventure started
   c event happened
   d journey began.

4 手紙をはこぶふくろう means:
   a a mouse who carries letters
   b an owl who carries letters
   c a cat who carries letters
   d a snake who carries letters.

5 The critic suggests that it is a good idea to:
   a read the book and see the movie at the same time
   b read the book after you have seen the movie
   c read the book before you see the movie.

49 Expressing uncertainty

AB 115(1)

Certainty
きっと —————— 90% sure
おそらく —————— 70%
たぶん —————— 50%
Optional

Probably, perhaps, maybe, I bet

Noun です	
な adjective です	でしょう (だろう plain form)
Verb dictionary form	or
い adj. plain form	かもしれません / かもしれない

Note: Always use かもしれません when talking about yourself rather than でしょう.
Don't combine きっと or おそらく with かもしれません. You can use たぶん.

れい

(きっと) あの人は中国人でしょう。	I bet that person is Chinese.
(たぶん) あしたは雨がふるでしょう。	Maybe it will rain tomorrow.
週まつは (おそらく) あついでしょう。	It's likely to be hot on the weekend.
(たぶん) 私も大学に行くかもしれません。	Perhaps I too can go to university.

Note: でしょう and だろう (the plain form) are very frequently used in conversation.
This is because Japanese people prefer not to sound too assertive.

Look at the pictures below and answer the following questions.

a　このはこの中に何があるのでしょうか。

b　デビーさんはどこに行ったん でしょうか。

あしたの天気よほう

AB 108

Listen to the weather forecast. What is forecast for the following cities?

a　Sapporo　　b　Sendai　　c　Tokyo　　d　Osaka

e　Matsuyama　f　Hiroshima　g　Fukuoka

CD2
track 23

上田先生、今日休みでしょう

Mr Ueda has not come to school today. Listen to his students' guesses as to the reason. Which guess is
most likely to be correct?

CD2
track 24

日本のアニメについて

「アニメ」と聞いて、みなさんはどんなものをそうぞうしますか？－「ディズニー映画、どうぶつ、ロボット、子供むけ」…？

日本では、「みやざき はやお」という映画かんとくがつくったアニメーション映画がとても人気があります。たとえば、「となりのトトロ (My Neighbour Totoro)」「もののけひめ (Princess Mononoke)」。これらの映画は、えいぞうがとてもきれいです。また、いろいろかんきょう問題としゃかい問題をテーマにしているから、子供だけでなく、大人も楽しむことができます。

このほか、「ポケモン」、「ドラゴンボール」など、日本のアニメは海外でも人気があります。日本のアニメは「ジャパニメーション (Japanimation)」ともよばれています。

「ポケモン」は子供達に人気があるアニメです。きいろくてかわいい「ピカチュー」というキャラクターがいろいろなぼうけんをします。ふつう、アニメは大きくてつよそうなキャラクターがヒーローですが、「ポケモン」のヒーローはかわいい「ピカチュー」です。「ピカチュー」は、おこるとすごいひかりをだしてヒーローになります。また、「ポケモン」は、映画やテレビで見るだけでなく、ゲームのキャラクターとしてもあそぶことができます。だから、世界の子供達に人気があるのかもしれません。

わかりましたか

1 Why are movies directed by Hayao Miyazaki popular with adults in Japan?
2 Why is Pokemon popular with children all over the world?
3 Write about an anime film you have seen.

たんご

えいぞう ⑦	images	そうぞうする	imagine
おこる	get angry	～だけでなく	not only
かいがい (海外)	overseas	ひかり	light
かんきょう	environment	ふつう	normally
かんとく	director	ぼうけん	adventure
そのほか	apart from this	～むけ	suitable for
しゃかい	society, social	もんだい	problem, issue
		よばれる ③	be called

千と千尋の神かくし
せん　ち ひろ　かみ

Spirited Away　AB 111

あらすじ

ちひろは 10 才の女の子。学校の友達とわかれて、新しい町にひっこしをする。そのと中、ふしぎなところにまよいこむ。お父さんとお母さんは、そこのごちそうをたくさん食べて、ぶたになった！ さあ、たいへん。お父さんとお母さんをたすけたい。でも、たすけ方がわからない。ちひろは、勇気 をだして、近くのたてものにはいっていく。そこで、ちひろのチャレンジがはじまる。
ゆう き

おすすめします

この映画は、小さい女の子の勇気と友情の物語です。小さくてよわい女の子でも、勇気と意志の力で何でもできるということを私達におしえてくれ
い し
ちから
ます。この映画は、おもしろいだけけではなく、見た後に元気がわいてきます。子どもも大人も楽しむことができます。

> **?**
>
> どの映画がみたい？
> スリラー？
> コメディー？
> アクション？
> ロマンス？

わかりましたか

1　Find these words and phrases:
  a　parted from her friends
  b　move house
  c　turned into pigs
  d　got lost in a strange place
  e　want to save
  f　I recommend to you (the critic's opinion)

2　What does 勇気 mean?
　　　　　　ゆう き
  a　energy
  b　courage
  c　faith

3　What does 友情 mean?
　　　　　　ゆうじょう
  a　friendship
  b　friendliness
  c　friends

4　What does 意志の力 mean?
　　　　　　い し　ちから
  a　happiness
  b　helpfulness
  c　willpower

5　What is the critic's opinion of this film?

6　What audiences is the film suitable for?

Kabuki

Kabuki is Japanese traditional theatre. It is said to have begun more than 350 years ago with the dance dramas of a woman dancer called Okuni. Her dances, which were initially performed by women and boys, were very popular. However, the Tokugawa Shogunate, which was the military government at that time, considered that Okuni's entertainment corrupted public morals and so female actors were banned. The dance dramas therefore came to be performed entirely by male actors, as they are today. The actors who play female parts are known as onnagata and are said to be so skilled at impersonating women that they are able to capture the very essence of femininity. The stories presented in the dramas are well

known to the audiences. There are three main types: historical dramas, dance dramas and domestic dramas. It is usual for a performance to consist of a number of dramas of each type. The Kabuki plays are characterised by extremely complex stage effects, fantastic costumes and intriguing dances. At dramatic moments in the play the leading characters strike a pose called a Mie. They glare at the audience and appear to slightly cross their eyes. This Mie vividly expresses the emotion of the character. Unlike conventional theatres, the actors in a Kabuki play often enter and exit along a platform built right through the audience, called the Hanamichi. Some of the action also takes place on the Hanamichi, right in the midst of the audience. This idea has often been copied in productions of modern plays. Foreigners can usually obtain a synopsis of the play in English and other European languages.

50 Asking what something is

AB 114

Unknown thing	というのは何ですか or simply って何ですか。

（れい）

こけしというのは何ですか。　　What is kokeshi?

すしって何ですか。　　What is sushi?

Note: Never say すしは何ですか.

ジョンくん、かぶきはおもしろい！？

AB 110(3)

わかりましたか

Find the following expressions.

1 … Japanese traditional art   3 … beautiful dancing   5 An incredible crowd

2 … wonderful costumes   4 Please take me with you   6 … extremely popular

わかりましたか

1 What impresses John about an onnagata?
2 What kind of things do the onnagata practise?
3 What does John think of the make-up?

わかりましたか

Why does John become embarrassed?

Kanji	Reading	Meaning		A way to remember
飲	の (む) イン	to drink		After 食 eating, open your mouth 欠 before you **drink**.
映	うつ (る) エイ	to be reflected		The 日 shines on a 人 person **reflected** in a shop window.
画	カク ガ	strokes (of a letter), picture		A **picture** is in a frame.
同	おな (じ) ドウ	the same		一 one 口 mouth under the same hood.
石	いし セキ	stone		厂 a cliff and a **stone**, which has rolled down.
有	あ (る) ユウ	exist, have		If you fly to the 月 moon you will be **famous**.
近	ちか (い) ちか (くに) キン	near, nearby		With this huge caterpillar **near**, you need an axe to protect yourself.

Compounds

How many meanings can you guess?

飲み水	のみみず	飲食	いんしょく	映画	えいが
画家	がか	同時	どうじ	同名	どうめい
石川	いしかわ	石山	いしやま	有名	ゆうめい
近海	きんかい	近所	きんじょ	近道	ちかみち

Look at the class reunion photo taken last week when last year's Year 12 students got together. The students in the picture are all talented in various ways and decided to try their luck in the entertainment industry. しゃくはち chatted to the first four in the picture, while びわ chatted to the last four.

They both learned some surprising things.

Take turns to be びわ and しゃくはち, giving your opinion about these imaginary people and telling each other what you heard, using patterns such as:

> …そうです。
> きっと / おそらく / たぶん …でしょう。or かもしれません。

（れい）

しゃくはち： メリッサは先月、ハリウッドへ行ったそうです！ たぶん、映画スターになるんでしょう。いいですね…

びわ： そうですか。すばらしいですね。マークはね、ディスクジョッキーになりたいそうです。今、ウエイターのしごとをしているそうです。土曜日のよるはとてもいそがしいそうです。お金がたくさんあるでしょうね。いいねえ…

（ヒント）

You could use the following words in your conversation.

えいがスター	movie star	ディスクジョッキー	disc jockey
はいゆう	actor	ポップシンガー	pop singer
タレント	TV celebrity	ロックシンガー	rock singer
しゅじんこう	heroine, hero	フォークシンガー	folk singer
アナウンサー	announcer	オペラかしゅ	opera singer
キャスター	newscaster	かしゅ	vocalist

チェックしましょう

千と千尋の神かくし

いし (意志)	will
おすすめします	I recommend to you (polite)
げんき (元気) がわく ⓤ	to become high-spirited
すすめる ⓡ	to recommend, advise
たすける ⓡ	to save
たてもの	building
ちから (力)	power, strength
とちゅう	on the way
ひっこしを する	to move house
ふしぎ [な]	strange, mysterious
ぶた	pig
まよいこむ ⓤ	to get lost
見たあと	after seeing it
ものがたり (物語)	story, tale
ゆうき (勇気)	courage
ゆうじょう (友情)	friendship
よわい	weak
わ (分) かれる ⓡ	to be parted

ハリー・ポッター

あらすじ	outline, the gist
いし (石)	stone
うれる ⓡ	to be sold, sell
えいぞう	image
まほう	magic
まほうつかい (使い)	magician, wizard
まもる ⓤ	to protect
ふくろう	owl

ジョンくん、かぶきはおもしろい?!

いしょう	costumes
おかしい	funny, amusing
おどり	dance
おんな (女) らしい	feminine
かぶきのけん	ticket for the kabuki
げいじゅつ	art
けしょう	make-up
つれていく (行く) ⓤ	to take with you (person)
でんとうてき [な]	traditional
なく ⓤ	to cry, weep
ばめん	scene
ひとごみ (人ごみ)	crowd of people

I can:
- discuss popular music
- describe the way of doing something
- say that things are the same
- read and understand an article about anime
- understand film critiques
- invite someone to a movie
- ask and talk about past experiences
- express uncertainty
- understand the use of 〜てしまう
- ask what something is
- understand and write the following kanji 飲 同 映 画 石 近 有

しゃかいとかんきょうの もんだい
Social and environmental issues

4
part

In these three units you will learn how to:
- discuss graffiti, recycling and the environment
- discuss bullying and ways to combat it
- discuss water conservation
- express your feelings about the environment.

Contents

10

かんきょうをまもるために
To protect the environment

らくがき

AB 120–121

ぼく達の高校のよこのかべに、だれかがひどいらくがきをしはじめました。高校のよこの道は、くらくてせまいから、あまり人が通りません。だから、らくがきをしやすいのかもしれません。でも、ぼく達にはとてもめいわくです。

さいきん、けいさつの人もこのきんじょをパトロールしはじめましたが、まだとめることはできません。時々、市やくしょの人が来てけしてくれますが、つぎの日にはまた新しいらくがきがあります。

みなさんの町では、同じようなもんだいはありませんか。らくがきがなくなるように、みんなでちからをあわせなければならないと思いますが、どうしたらいいでしょうか。何か、いいかんがえがありませんか。みなさんのいけんが聞きたいです。

わかりましたか

1 Why does the writer think that it is easy for people to do graffiti in this area?

2 How do the writer and friends feel about the graffiti?

3 What has been tried to stop the graffiti appearing?

4 How successful was this?

5 What does the writer ask the reader to do?

らくがきをとめるため

Here are some ways in which cities have tackled the graffiti problem. Put the suggestions in the order that you think would be the most successful in your area.

1 市やくしょの人がすぐにらくがきをけしに来る。

2 らくがき用のかべをつくる。

3 らくがきをした人が、かべをきれいにしなければならない。

4 らくがきをした人は、そのかべやビルのもちぬしと話をしなければならない。

5 らくがきは、そのかべやビルのもちぬしが、すぐにけさなければならない。

6 らくがきをする人がびじゅつ大学に行くのを市やくしょが、たすける。

らくがきクイズ

正しいこたえをえらんでください。

1　らくがきは
　　a　私のもんだいじゃない。けいさつのもんだいだ。
　　b　はんざいだ。
　　c　ただの子どものゲームだ。

2　らくがきをする人は
　　a　やくざだけ
　　b　子どもだけ
　　c　いろいろな人。とくにティーンエージャーから 25 才くらいまでの人が多い。

3　らくがきをする人は
　　a　えを上手に書きたいから、れんしゅうしている。
　　b　白いかべはつまらないから、えやメッセージを書いてかざっている。
　　c　社会にたいするはんこうの気持ちと自分のパワーをあらわしたい。

こたえはつぎのページ

51 Begin/finish doing something

verb ます	+ はじめる	begin 〜
	+ おわる	finish 〜

れい

去年、中国語を勉強しはじめた。

I began to study Chinese last year.

先週、ギターをならいはじめた。

I began to learn the guitar last week.

弟はごちそうを見て、食べはじめた。

My brother saw the feast and started eating.

この本は、きのうのよる読みおわったんです。

I finished reading this book last night.

宿題をしおわって、先生に E メールをした。

I finished the homework and emailed it to the teacher.

兄は十時に車をあらいおわった。

My brother finished washing the car at 10 o'clock.

Match each half-sentence in column A with a suitable ending from column B. Rewrite the completed sentence in English in your notebook.

Column A
1　さちこさんは手紙を書きおわって、
2　空がくらくなって、
3　あした、レポートを
4　みんな、宿題をやりおわったから、
5　去年、日本語を

Column B
a　うちにかえってもいいです。
b　勉強しはじめました。
c　ゆうびんきょくに行きました。
d　雨がふりはじめました。
e　書きはじめたいと思います。

---

52 Is easy to do/is hard to do

verb ます	+ やすい	is easy to …
	+ にくい	is hard to …

れい

人というかんじはかきやすいですね。　The kanji 人 is easy to write.

このステーキは食べにくいですね。　This steak is hard to eat, isn't it?

Note: The addition やすい or にくい to the verb stem changes the word into an
い adjective which can change in the same way as い adjectives. For example:
かきやすくない not easy to write, よみにくくなかった it was not difficult to read.

1　Make dialogues using the following example as a guide.

れい

新しいくつ　　小さい　　はく

新しいくつはどうですか。　　　　　How are the new shoes?

小さくて はきにくいです。　　　　They are small and (so are) hard to wear.

- **a** 先生のせつめい　ながい　分かる
- **b** そのじしょ　じが　小さい　読む
- **c** このコンピューター　ふくざつ　使う
- **d** このくすり　にがい　のむ
- **e** このふるいビデオ　音がわるい　聞く

2　Make dialogues using the following example as a guide.

れい

新しい家　広い　住む

新しい家は どう？　　　　　　　　How is the new house?

広くて住みやすいよ。　　　　　　　It is spacious and easy to live in. (comfortable)

- **a** あのジーンズ　大きい　はく
- **b** ペンパルの手紙　かんたん　読む
- **c** 新しい車　オートマチック　うんてんする
- **d** イタリア語　ことばが　やさしい　おぼえる
- **e** ふじ山　いい　道がある　のぼる

らくがきクイズのこたえ
1 b, 2 c, 3 c

53 Describing people or things using relative clauses with verbs

descriptive sentence verb in plain form	person or thing	rest of sentence

れい

らくがきをした人が かべをきれいにしなければなりません。

The people who did the graffiti should clean it off.

赤いセーターをきている女の子が サリーです。

The girl who is wearing the red sweater is Sally.

来週のキャンプに行かない人は 五人います。

There are five people who are not going to next week's camp.

Note: Relative clauses in English come after the noun which they describe and start with *which, that, who, where*. For example: The cat <u>which ate the mouse</u> is John's. In Japanese the descriptive clause comes before the topic so this sentence becomes <u>ねずみを食べた</u>ねこはジョンくんのねこです。

Constructing sentences with relative clauses

Here is a simple sentence.

マリーさんはみせでざっしを買いました。

Marie bought a magazine in the shop.

You can add a description of Marie, the magazine and the shop.

<u>日本語ができる</u>マリーさんは、<u>えきのとなりにある</u>みせで、<u>日本について書いてある</u>ざっしを買いました。

Marie, who can read Japanese, bought a magazine, which is about Japan, at the shop, which is next to the station.

Add relative clauses to the underlined Japanese nouns so that the sentences have the same meaning as the English translation.

1 <u>人</u>はとても少ない。
   The people <u>who don't have mobile phones</u> are very few.

2 <u>子ども</u>はだれですか。
   Who is the child <u>crying over there</u>?

3 <u>女の子</u>はゆかりさんです。
   The girl <u>who is talking to Mr Tanaka</u> is Yukari.

4 <u>けんくん</u>はえいごがじょうずです。
   Ken, w<u>ho came from Japan last month</u>, speaks English well.

5 <u>男の子</u>は十才です。
   The boy <u>who did the graffiti</u> is 10 years old.

リサイクル Recycling

Sachiko visits her friend Thomas

In your notebook, indicate if the following statements are TRUE (T) or FALSE (F). Give reasons for F answers.

1 Thomas is about to plant a jacaranda tree.
2 Sachiko thinks that the large bin is a compost bin.
3 Thomas explains that apart from vegetable and fruit peelings, they add soil to the compost.
4 Sachiko says that in Japan they recycle newspaper, glass, bottles, aluminium and steel cans.
5 Sachiko said that people take their own plastic bags when they go to the supermarket.

イディオム

おじゃまします literally means 'I am disturbing you'. It is used as a greeting when visiting someone in their home or office. It is like an apology for intruding. The reply to おじゃまします is いらっしゃい, which means 'Welcome'.

いらっしゃい can also be said first and おじゃまします is then the reply. When leaving it is usual to say おじゃましました. (Sorry to have taken up your time.)

54 Expressing having just done something

Verb plain past	+	ところです

れい

朝ご飯を 食べた ところです。　　　　I have just finished eating breakfast.
おふろに はいった ところですよ。　　　I have just got into the bath!

Complete the following dialogues with a suitable response using 〜た ところです.

1 たろう：　もしもし、たろうですが、カレンさんおねがいします。
　　カレン：　ああ！ たろうさん、こんばんは。あなたに手紙を ＿＿＿＿＿＿＿＿

2 トム：　　おじゃまします。
　　さちこ：　あ、トム。いらっしゃい。今あなたに電話 ＿＿＿＿＿＿＿＿

3 母：　　　さちこ、あしたビーチのクリーン・アップだよ。知ってる？
　　さちこ：　ええ、知っているわ。新聞で ＿＿＿＿＿＿＿＿

4 さぶろう：　おなかがすいた。
　　デビー：　あ、今 ケーキを ＿＿＿＿＿＿＿＿ いっしょに食べましょう。

分かりましたか

Find these expressions in the cartoon on page 154.

1   Such a waste, isn't it?
2   We must do something …
3   I think we have to stop the waste of paper.
4   After working and trying hard …
5   It's a great feeling.

55 Expressing purpose, in order to, for the sake of   AB 123, 127

noun の	+ ため (に)
verb dictionary form	

れい

かんきょうの ために木をたくさんうえましょう。

Let's plant lots of trees for (the sake of) the environment.

ごみをへらすために いろいろなものを リサイクルしている。

In order to reduce rubbish, we are recycling various things.

かんきょうを まもるために何かしなきゃ。

We must do something (in order) to protect the environment.

Note: In English the idea of purpose does not always appear in words.

Match the sentence on the left with a suitable ending on the right.

1   けんこうのために…   a   お金をためています。
2   おじにあうために…   b   かがくをしっかり勉強しています。
3   日本語のテストにパスするために…   c   たばこをやめます。
4   日本へ行くために…   d   アメリカへ行きます。
5   いしゃになるために…   e   かんじを勉強します。

If you want to say 'In order to be able to do something, don't use ために. ように is used instead, for example 日本へ行くことができるように お金をためています。

56 Expressing make an effort to, make it a rule to ... not to ...

verb dictionary form
verb plain negative

+ ように します

れい

電車を使うように しています。　I am making an effort to use trains.

みせへ ぬのぶくろを もっていくようにするよ。

I will make it a rule to carry a cloth bag to the store.

物を むだづかい しない ように しましょう。

Let's make an effort not to waste things.

1　Complete the following dialogues using the phrases provided. Add the appropriate form of ようにする.

　　a　母：　　今年、雨がふらなくて、たいへんね。

　　　　雪子：　ええ、私達はお水を ＿＿＿＿＿＿＿＿＿＿ (たいせつに使う)

　　b　先生：　学校のきょうしつはとてもきたなくなったね。毎日、おべんとうの後で

　　　　　　　ごみを ＿＿＿＿＿＿＿＿＿ (ひろう) なければならないよ。

　　　　せいと：すみません、ごみはごみばこに ＿＿＿＿＿＿＿＿＿ (いれる)

　　c　いしゃ：田中さんは、もうすこしうんどうをしなければなりませんね。

　　　　田中：　はい、先生。毎日 2 キロぐらい ＿＿＿＿＿＿＿＿＿ (あるく)

2　Write an essay entitled かんきょうをまもるために何ができるかな？

かんきょうのインタビュー

1　List, in Japanese, what each of the people interviewed are doing to protect the environment.

2　Think about each person's efforts and decide on the order of importance of their efforts. Write your decisions in English.

Kanji	Reading	Meaning		A way to remember
使	つか (う) シ	to use		人 a person has a length of rope cut into + 10 pieces. He tells with his 口 mouth how to **use** it.
黒	くろ (い) コク	black		A spray can has sprayed four drops of black paint.
書	か (く) ショ	to write		A brush held in the hand, a weight to keep the paper still while you **write**.
去	さ (る) キョ	to go away, past		土 earth is on top of the elbow of a buried statue from the **past**.
道	みち ドウ	road, path		Someone wearing a big hat hides from a huge caterpillar on the **road**.
広	ひろ (い) コウ	wide, spacious		The sumo restler can only get his elbow into this cave. It should be more **spacious**.
知	し (る) し (らせる) チ	to know to let know		人 a person with a short leg shelters under an awning. His open 口 mouth lets you **know**.

Compounds

AB 125

How many meanings can you guess?

使い方	つかいかた	黒板	こくばん	白黒	しろくろ
書道	しょどう	書体	しょたい	去年	きょねん
水道	すいどう	柔道	じゅうどう	道具	どうぐ
広大	こうだい	広々	ひろびろ	知人	ちじん

CD2
track 33

This account of one man's fight to clean up the environment appeared in a Japanese newspaper.

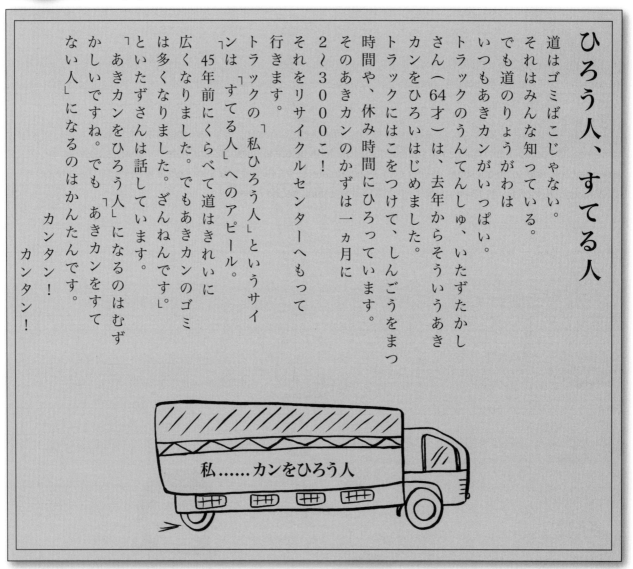

ひろう人、すてる人

道はゴミばこじゃない。

それはみんな知っている。

でも道のりょうがわはいつもあきカンがいっぱい。

トラックのうんてんしゅ、いたずたかしさん（64才）は、去年からそういうあきカンをひろいはじめました。

トラックにはこをつけて、しんごうをまつ時間や、休み時間にひろっています。

そのあきカンのかずは一ヵ月に2～300こ！

それをリサイクルセンターへもって行きます。

トラックの「私ひろう人」というサインは「すてる人」へのアピール。

45年前にくらべて道はきれいに広くなりました。でもあきカンのゴミは多くなりました。ざんねんです！

といたずさんは話しています。

「あきカンをひろう人」になるのはむずかしいですね。でも「あきカンをすてない人」になるのはかんたんです。

カンタン！

カンタン！

私......カンをひろう人

分かりましたか

1 a What does Mr Itazu do to improve his environment?

  b How successful has he been?

  c Why does he put a sign on his truck?

2 Prepare a dialogue between Mr Itazu and a TV interviewer.

3 Write a letter of protest to the paper.

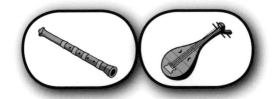

In this activity you and your partner will take turns to play the roles of a young Japanese tourist and an interviewer.

しゃくはち: You are the tourist. Write the details of your assumed personality in your notebook, using the headings in the form below. Read the statements on the form and decide to what degree いつも ーぜんぜん you agree with them. Write the number of the statement and your opinion in your notebook. Answer the interviewer's questions.

びわ: Your job is to interview Japanese tourists to find out how environmentally aware they are. First find out the person's name, age and occupation. Change the statements on the form below to questions and note the tourist's answers in your notebook. Add some questions of your own. Congratulate しゃくはち if you think he/she is trying too hard to be environmentally friendly. Try to persuade しゃくはち if you think he/she is not.

Tourist details

名前：　　　　　（　才)：　　　　しごと：				
1 買い物に行く時 ぬのぶくろを もっていきます。	a いつも	b よく	c 時々	d ぜんぜん
2 コーラなどのアルミカンを リサイクルします。	a いつも	b よく	c 時々	d ぜんぜん
3 あきカンを ひろって ごみばこに いれます。	a いつも	b よく	c 時々	d ぜんぜん
4 木を うえたことがあります。	a はい	b いいえ		
5 友達やしんせきの人とビーチのクリーンアップを したことがあります。	a はい	b いいえ		

チェックしましょう AB 130–131

らくがき

あわせる ③	to combine
きんじょ	neighbourhood
くらい	dark
けす ⑤	to erase
しやくしょ (市やくしょ)	city hall
せまい	narrow
たすける ③	to help, assist
どうしたらいい	what shall we do?
ひどい	dreadful
めいわく	annoyance
もちぬし	owner
～よう (用)	for ～
よこ	side, next to
～ように	so as to

リサイクル

うえる ③	to plant, sow, grow
かわ	skin, peel, rind, crust
しんぶんし (新聞紙)	old newspaper
そうしたら	if you do it that way
～ために	in order to
ぬのぶくろ	cloth bags
バケツ	bucket
ビニールぶくろ	plastic bags
へらす ⑤	to decrease, reduce
まもる ⑤	to protect, guard
むだづかい	extravagance, waste
むらさき	purple
もったいない	what a waste

ひろう人 すてる人

あきかん (空きかん)	empty can
うんてんしゅ	driver
かず	number
かんたん	simple, easy
すてる ③	to throw away
ひろう ⑤	to pick up, gather up
りょうがわ	both sides

らくがきクイズ

あらわす ⑤	to show, indicate
けいさつ	police
しゃかい	society
たいする	towards
ただ	only, merely
はんこう	opposition, rebellion
はんざい	crime
やくざ	gangster

I can:
- discuss graffiti
- say something is easy/hard to do
- discuss recycling
- express purpose
- express 'make an effort to'
- comprehend an article about cleaning up Japan's roadsides
- recognise and write the following kanji
  使 書 黒 去 道 広 知

Unit 11

いじめ
Bullying

どうしたらいいのでしょう

AB 133–134

CD2
track 35–37

A Japanese website offers counselling to troubled students. The following letters were published on the website recently, written by students who were being bullied at school.

A: 中学 1 年生・男子

AB 135A

ぼくは中学 1 年生です。ぼくのあだなは「かべ」です。クラスメイトはいつもぼくを「かべ」とよびます。何か言おうとすると、「かべはしゃべってはいけない。」と言います。またクラスメイトはぼくをたたきます。ぼくはぼうりょくがきらいだから、たたかれても何もしません。すると、クラスメイトは「かべは手がないんだから、何もするな。」と言います。今ではクラスのみんながぼくを「かべ」とよんで、わらいます。「かべは動かないものだ」と言って、ほかのあそびやスポーツにもぼくはくわえてもらえません。ぼくは、どうしたらいいのでしょう。

わかりましたか

1   Find these expressions in the letter and write them in Japanese in your notebook.
    a   I don't do anything
    b   Walls are not allowed to chat
    c   I hate violence so
    d   They won't let me take part
    e   When I try to say something

2   Answer the following questions.
    a   What is the writer's nickname?
    b   In what ways do the writer's classmates torment him?
    c   What does the writer do to stop these things happening?
    d   How serious do you consider this situation is?

Level of seriousness:

Not serious				Extremely serious
1	2	3	4	5

B: 中学 2 年生・女子

私はアメリカで小学校をそつぎょうして、日本に帰ってきました。日本の中学校に入ってから、じゅ
ぎょう中に、わからないことを手を上げて先生に聞くと、クラスのみんなが「ああー」とためいきをつ
きます。また、じゅぎょう中に先生のしつもんに私がこたえると、クラスのみんなが「ああー」とため
いきをつきます。先生はクラスのみんなに、私が帰国子女だから、なかよくしなさいと言います。で
も、先生がそう言うと、クラスのみんなはもっと大きいこえで「ああー」と言います。先生は私に、
「あなたはアメリカの小学校に行っていたから、日本のことはわかりにくいでしょうね。でも、ここは
日本なのです。日本のやり方でやるように、どりょくするのも大事ですよ。」と言います。でも、日本の
やり方って、何でしょう。しつもんをしたり、いけんを言ったりするのは、どうしていけないのでしょう。

わかりましたか

1 Find these expressions in the letter and write them in
   Japanese in your notebook.
   a When I ask the teacher
   b graduated from primary school
   c let out a sigh
   d things I don't know
   e do it the Japanese way
   f when I answer
   g because she has come back from overseas
   h why is it wrong?
   i be good friends

2 What does the class do to upset this student?
3 How does the teacher react?
4 How serious do you consider this situation to be?

Level of seriousness:

	Not serious				Extremely serious
	1	2	3	4	5

C: 高校 1 年生・男子

ぼくはアジアのある国で生まれました。りょうしんもその国の人です。日本に来て、もう 5 年がたちました。日本語もだいぶわかるようになりました。でも、時々「くさい」「きたない」「バイキン、あっち行け」と言われます。ぼくの学校はせいふくがなくて、しふくで行きます。ぼくの家はあまりお金がないから、同じふくを着て学校へ行きます。でも、ぼくは毎日おふろに入っていて、毎日下着もかえています。どうして「くさい」と言われるのか、わかりません。この前、教室へ行くと、ぼくのつくえは教室の一番うしろのすみになっていて、かばんはごみばこに入れられていました。クラスのみんなは「ちかづくな」「さわるな」とぼくに言います。ぼくはアジア人だから、いじめやすいのでしょうか。くやしいです。もう学校へ行かないつもりです。

わかりましたか

1 Find these expressions and write them in Japanese in your notebook.
a humiliating
b furthest corner
c never come near!
d Never touch us!
e change underwear
f stinking
g was pushed in
h germ
i Go back!
j I don't know why I am called 'Kusai'.

2 What do the students call this student?
3 How else do they torment him?
4 Why do you think they pick on him?
5 How serious do you consider this situation is?

Level of seriousness:

Not serious				Extremely serious
1	2	3	4	5

57 If/when you do this, something happens

| verb dictionary form | と | outcome |

(れい)

まっすぐ行くと、学校が見えます。

If you go straight ahead, you can see the school.

私がこたえると、みんなが「ああー」とためいきをつきます。

When I answer, everyone lets out a sigh.

先生がそう言うと、みんなは大きなこえで「ああー」と言います。

When the teacher says this, eveyone says a big 'Aah'.

教室に行くと、ぼくのつくえはすみになっていました。

When I went to the classroom, my desk was in the corner.

1　Choose a suitable ending from column B to complete the sentence beginnings in column A.

Write your completed sentences in your notebook and give the meaning in English of each sentence.

Column A

このくすりを飲むと、

えきに着くと、

ファミコンのゲームをやりすぎると、

このボタンをおすと、

このうたを聞くと、

先生がきょうしつに入ってくると、

Column B

すぐに電車が来ました。

おどりたくなるんです。

みんなしずかになりました。

目がわるくなります。

元気になります。

ドアがあきます。

2　Read the following cause-and-effect passage and with a partner write a new version.

冬になると、みんなはたらきません。

冬になると、さむくなります。さむくなると、雪がふります。雪がふると、山に食べ物がなくなります。山に食べ物がなくなると、さるはおなかがすきます。さるはおなかがすくと、よる、山からおりて、人のにわに来ます。よる、さるが人のにわに来ると、いぬがなきます。よる、いぬがなくと、みんなねることができません。よる、ねることができないと、ひるまにねむくなります。ひるまにねむくなると、みんなはたらきません。

イディオム

Strong and abrupt imperatives (commands) were used in the passages about bullying. In conversation, these sound very rude and offensive and you should not use them.

Positive and negative imperatives

(れい)

あっち行け！	Go away!	話せ！	Speak up!
しゃべるな！	No talking!	ちかづくな！	Never come near us!

どうしたらいいのでしょう。This means 'What shall I do?' It literally means: 'What thing if I do it will be good I wonder?'

58 Expressing intentions

1	verb dictionary form or ない form	+ つもりです	I intend to … I intend not to … (I don't intend to …)

2	verb dictionary form	+ つもりはありません	I have no intention of

れい

来年 中国語をべんきょうするつもりです。　Next year I intend to study Chinese.

もうたばこを すわないつもりです。　I intend not to smoke any more.

もうあそこへ行くつもりはありません。　I have no intention of going there any more.

Using the topics below, make dialogues like the following:

れい

夏休み　アルバイトをする　　　　　　友だちとキャンプに行く

A: 夏休みに何をするつもりですか。

What are you planning to do in the summer holidays?

B: アルバイトをするつもりです。あなたは？

I intend to get a part-time job. How about you?

A: 友だちとキャンプに行くつもりです。

I'm going camping with friends.

B: ああ、うらやましいですね。

Oh, you are lucky, aren't you?

1 しゅうまつ　映画を見る　　　　　ロックコンサートに行く
2 こんばん　洗たくをする　　　　　ファミコンをする
3 ほうかご きょうしつをそうじする　バスケットボールのれんしゅうをする
4 日曜日　宿題をする　　　　　　　新しいCDを聞く
5 来年　同じかもくを勉強する　　　ファッションモデルになる

新しい学校はどう？

Ken is phoning his friend Daigo. Pretend that you are Daigo.
Answer the following questions put to you by a mutual friend.
Write your answers in your notebook.

1 How is Ken feeling?

2 Why is feeling like this?

3 What do you think of the situation?

4 What did you advise him to do?

5 What do you plan to do in the future?

CD2 track 38

「いじめ」についてスキットを通してかんがえる！《一番いいたいしょのしかたは？》

「いじめ」には、おす、たたく、ののしる、むしするなどある。ほかに、人種さべつてきなことを言う、悪口を言うなどの「いじめ」もある。

クイーンズランドの4校のハイスクールで「いじめ」にたいしょする、とくべつきょういくがはじまった。生徒達は「いじめ」についてスキットを通してかんがえる。

生徒達はスキットの中で「いじめ」をえんじる。いじめる生徒のやくと、いじめられる生徒のやくを、こうたいしてえんじる。そして、どんなたいしょのしかたが一番いいか、みんなでかんがえるのだ。

上の学年が下の学年の前で、えんじることもある。それを見て、みんなはいじめられる生徒に同情しはじめる。そして、みんな大切なことに気がつく。それは、まわりで見ているだけでは、いじめているのと同じだということだ。

生徒達は、このプロジェクトを通して、「いじめ」を自分達のもんだいとして、かんがえはじめた。それは、どうするのがいいか、きめるのは大人ではなくて、自分達だからだ。

わかりましたか

Read the article above and answer the following questions.

1 What is the important thing that everyone has become aware of?

2 In what way does the project involve the whole school?

3 How have students' perceptions of 'ijime' changed?

たんご

いじめる ③	bully
いじめられる ③	be bullied
えんじる ③	perform, act
おす	push
かんがえる ③	consider
気がつく	become aware
きめる ③	decide
きょういく	education
こうたい ＜する＞	take turns
じんしゅ (人種) さべつ	racism
人種さべつてき [な]	racist

たいしょ する	tackle
大切 [な]	important
通して	through
～ということだ	is the fact that
同情 (どうじょう)	sympathy
とくべつ [な]	special
まわりで	around
むし ＜する＞	ignore
ののしる ⑤	verbal abuse
やく	role
わるくち (悪口) を言う ⑤	speak ill of

Kanji	Reading	Meaning		A way to remember
着	き (る) つ (く) チャク	to wear to arrive		A sheep 羊 provides wool for a sweater which we pull over our eyes 目 **to wear**.
教	おし (える) キョウ	to teach		Earth 土 linked to a child 子 by a cord and a CD-ROM, by which to **teach**.
室	むろ シツ	store room, room		Between the roof and the earth 土 there is one 一 katakana ム to show the **rooMU**.
動	うご (く) ドウ	to move		**To move** a 1000 千 spray paint cans takes a lot of strength 力.
帰	かえ (る) キ	to return (home)		Looks like katakana リ plus katakana yo(u) over a banner to welcome you home when you **return**.
国	くに コク	country		There is a border around this **country**. The king's crown jewels 玉 are in the centre.

Compounds

How many meanings can you guess?

水着	みずぎ	先着	せんちゃく	教会	きょうかい
教室	きょうしつ	音楽室	おんがくしつ	自動	じどう
自動車	じどうしゃ	帰国	きこく	国々	くにぐに

おばさん、私はどうしたらいいでしょうか。 AB 140

Mariko lives in Australia with her family. She wrote the following letter to her aunt.

おばちゃん、お元気ですか。ひさしぶりですね。こちらはみんな元気です。お母さんとお父さんは先週からスペインりょこうに行っていて、私は今一人です。ちょっとホームシックで、東京に帰りたくてたまりません。お母さんとお父さんはここに住みたいと言っているけど。

私は今年、いっしょうけんめい勉強しているんですよ。高校三年生ですからね！来年、大学に行って、かんきょうの勉強をしたいと思っています。

さいきん、お金がいりますから、毎週土曜日に、コーヒーショップでアルバイトをはじめました。時給はすごく安くて8ドルです。一日に三時間ぐらい、はたらいています。このアルバイトが…ちょっともんだいなんです。

だいたい、三人が店ではたらいています。一人がちゅうもんをとって、二人がコーヒーやサンドイッチをつくります。オーナーはすごくきびしくていじわるなんです。たとえば、私はいつもおさらやグラスをせんざいであらう時、水をながしてすすいでいます。オーナーがこれを見て「そんなことはしなくてもいい。時間と水のむだだ！」と言いました。「でも、せんざいは体にわるいと思います。」と言うと、時給を7ドルしかはらってくれませんでした。ひどいでしょう？オーナーはよく私にどなったりします。私は日本人だから、いじめやすいのでしょうか。くやしいです。

先週、ちょっとじけんがありました。みせの前のボードがなくなったんです。オーナーは私に「ばかやろう」とどなりました。私がみせの前を見ていなかったからだ、と言いました。でも、どうやって、サンドイッチをつくっている時に、みせの前も見ることができるでしょう？オーナーは、私が新しいボードを買わなければならないと言っています。新しいボードは100ドルぐらいだそうです。私は毎週、24ドルぐらいしかもらっていません。おばさん、私はどうしたらいいでしょうか。

まり子より

わかりましたか

1 Why is Mariko living on her own at present?
2 What difference of opinion does she have with her parents?
3 What are her plans for the future?
4 What kind of part-time work has she begun to do?
5 What kind of person is her employer? Explain why you think so.
6 Why has she written this letter to her aunt?
7 Guess the meaning of the underlined words.

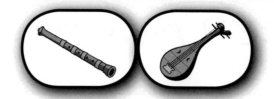

Take turns to play the part of student and teacher.

しゃくはち: You are the teacher. One of your students has come to talk to you.

びわ: You are student A on page 161. Tell your teacher what has been happening to you. You could start this way:

先生:　　　どうしたんですか。

びわ:　　　クラスメイトはいつもぼくを「かべ」とよぶんです。

先生:　　　そうか。どうして「かべ」とよぶの？

びわ:　　　わかりません。

先生:　　　そう、ひどいですね。

びわ:　　　はい、それに、しゃべってはいけないと言います。… continue telling what happens to you at school.

You could finish this way:

せんせい:　そうか。しんぱいしないで。明日、クラスのみんなと話すから。

This time びわ is the teacher. One of your students, an Indian boy, has come to talk to you.

しゃくはち: You are student C on page 163. Tell your teacher what has been happening to you. You could start this way:

先生:　　　　　どうしたんですか。

しゃくはち:　クラスメイトはいつも ぼくを「くさい」「きたない」「バイキン」とよびます。

先生:　　　　　そうか。どうしてそんなことを言うの？。

しゃくはち:　わかりません。毎日、おふろに入っていて、… (continue telling about your home life)

先生:　　　　　そうか。クラスメイトはほかに、どんなことをするの？

しゃくはち:　よく「あっちへ行け」と言います。… (continue telling what happens to you at school).

You could finish this way:

せんせい:　そうか。話してくれてよかったよ。みんなのりょうしんと話してみるから、しんぱいしないで。

チェックしましょう

どうしたらいいのでしょう。A

あだな	nickname
いじめ	bullying
うごく (動く) ⓤ	move
くわえる ⓡ	add, include
しゃべる ⓤ	speak, chat
すると	and then
たたかれる ⓡ	be hit, beaten
たたく ⓤ	hit, beat
ぼうりょく	violence
ほかの	other
よぶ ⓤ	call
わらう ⓤ	laugh

どうしたらいいのでしょう。B

いけん	opinion
きこくしじょ (帰国子女)	returnee children
しつもん	questions
だいじ (大事)	important
ためいきをつく ⓤ	sigh
なかよくする	be friendly

おばさん、私はどうしたらいいでしょうか。

いじわる	bad-tempered, mean
くやしい	humiliating
じけん	incident, event
じきゅう (時給)	hourly pay
すすぐ ⓤ	rinse
せんざい	detergent
ちゅうもん する	order, to order
どなる ⓤ	yell at, growl
ながす ⓤ	let flow, pour away
ばかやろう	fool, idiot
はらう ⓤ	pay
ひさしぶり	it's a long time
むだ	waste
りょこう	travel, journey

どうしたらいいのでしょう。C

入れられる ⓡ	be put in
いわれる(言われる) ⓡ	be told
うまれる(生まれる) ⓡ	be born
くさい	stinking
くやしい	humiliating
さわる ⓤ	touch
すみ	corner
だいぶ	a great deal
たつ ⓤ	pass (time)
ちかづく (近づく) ⓤ	come near
バイキン	germs

I can:

- understand complaints about bullying
- understand an article about overcoming bullying
- express when/if
- express intentions
- understand a letter about workplace harassment
- understand a strong command using 'never', 'don't'
- read and write the following kanji
  帰 動 教 室 着 国

Unit 12

水のせつやく
Saving water

水を 大切に 使いましょう。
たいせつ

CD2
track 40

ふつうの 家ていで、一日 へいきん 500 リットルから 800 リットルの水を使います。
これは 大きい バケツに 65 はいから 100 ぱいです。こんなに たくさんの 水が
本当に ひつよう でしょうか？？
ほんとう

AB 143-144

---

1 じゃ口から 水もれ していませんか。
　チェックしましょう！

　こんなにせつやくできる。

---

2 はをみがいている 時、
　水を出していませんか？
　だ
　はみがきはコップ 1
　ぱいの水で 十分ですよ。
　じゅうぶん

　こんなにせつやくできる

---

3 車を洗う 時、バケツに水を
　あら
　ためて洗いましょう。ホースで
　水をながすのは たくさん
　水を使います。

　こんなにせつやくできる →

---

4 にわや家の前を水でそうじする
　のは よくないです。ほうきで
　そうじするほうがいいです。

　こんなにせつやくできる

水道の じゃ口から 一時間に 1000 リットルの 水が 出ます。よく かんがえて むだづかい しないよう
にしましょう。

分かりましたか

Can you guess the new words? Complete the following vocabulary list. Write it in your notebook.

か	家てい	household	な	ながす	let flow, run
さ	じゃ口		は	はをみがく	
	十分 (じゅうぶん)			ひつよう	
	すいどう (水道)			へいきん	
	せつやく			ほうき	
た	ためる		ま	みずもれ (水もれ)	

Noun の / だった な adjective な / だった い adjective plain form verb plain form	+ とき (に、は、には)

れい

はをみがいている時、水を出していませんか。

Don't you let the water run when you brush your teeth?

日本に行った時、かぶきを見に行った。

I went to see the kabuki when I went to Japan. (While I was there)

車を洗う時、水をむだづかいしないようにしましょう。

Let's not waste water when we wash the car.

もっとしずかな時に、またせつめいしてください。

Please explain again when it is quieter.

さむい時は、うちの中に いるのがいいです。

I prefer to be inside when it is cold.

小学生の時には、スポーツが きらいでしたが、今は 大好きです。

When I was in primary school I hated sport but now I love it.

Note:

1   The tense of adjectives and nouns + とき is sometimes in the present although the meaning may be in the past.

れい

小さい時 When I was small ... 高校生の時 When I was a high school student ...

2   There is little difference bertween 時 and 時に Both mean 'when'. Both 時は and 時には —'as for when'—suggest that there is a contrast between the time 'when' and now or in the future.

いつ ('when') is used only for asking questions.

Complete the sentences in column A by combining them with a suitable ending from column B.

Column A	Column B
1 雨の時に、	a ぬのぶくろをもって行くようにしましょう。
2 つまらない時は、	b ほうきでそうじするほうがいいです。
3 子どもの時に、	c コップ１ぱいの水で十分です。
4 この本を よんだ時、	d 気をつけましょう。
5 家の前をそうじする時は、	e よくビデオを見ます。
6 はみがきをする時は、	f じてんしゃに のってはいけません。
7 買い物に行く時は、	g かなしくなりました。
8 電車にのる時には、	h アフリカに住んでいました。

Kanji	Reading	Meaning		A way to remember
切	き (る) セツ	to cut, chop		With a 刀 sword, cut **into** 七 seven.
出	で (る) だ (す) シュツ	to go out, to appear, to put out, to post		山 山 Let's **go out** to the mountains.
入	はい (る) い (れる) ニュウ	to enter, go in, to put in, let in		人 a person is turning to the left to **put in** the other foot.
洗	あら (う) あら (い) セン	to wash, washing		The runner who forged ahead 先 needs water for a **wash**.
庭	にわ テイ	garden		A cliff 广 plus 王 king. The king is stretching his legs in the **garden**.
次	つぎ (に) つぎ (の) ジ	next, secondly, next, following		Only two drops of water for each open mouth. **Next** one.

Compounds

How many meanings can you guess?

大切	たいせつ	切手	きって	出口	でぐち
出金	しゅっきん	入り口	いりぐち	入れ物	いれもの
入学	にゅうがく	水洗	すいせん	洗濯	せんたく
次々	つぎつぎ	家庭	かてい	石庭	せきてい

水の使い方

―日本のアイデア―

日本の アイデアは オーストラリアの アイデアと ちがうと 思います。
私の ホストファミリーの 中むらさんの アイデアを しょうかいします。

a おふろは シャワーより、水を せつやくすることが できます。シャワーも 使いますが、シャワーをする 時間は みじかいです。

b おふろの おゆを すてないで、次の朝 洗たくに 使います。中むらさんの お母さんは 小さい ポンプを もっていました。

c トイレのタンクの 上で、手を 洗うことが できます。その後、水は タンクに はいります。

d おばあさんは いつも おこめを 洗って その水を 花や うえ木に やっていました。水道の 水より いいそうです。

分かりましたか

Discuss which of the above water-saving activities could be used in your town.

60 Expressing 'is different from'

| A は　B と | + | ちがいます | A is different from B |

| A と　B は | + | ちがいます | A and B are different |

れい

日本の アイデアは オーストラリアのアイデアと ちがいます。

Japanese ideas are different from Australian ideas.

このごみと あのごみは ちがいます。

This rubbish and that rubbish are different.

Complete the following sentences using と ちがう。
1　私の学校のこうそくは…
2　うちのコンピュータは…
3　クリケットのルールは…
4　日本のりょうりは…
5　かぶきと…

61 Expressing do … this way, not that way

| Sentence 1 verb ない form | + | で | sentence 2 |
| Not doing that | | | do this |

れい

おゆは すてないで 洗たくに 使うようにしましょう。

Don't throw away the hot water—make an effort to use it for the washing.

1　Combine the following sentences using ないで.
　a　せんざいは使いません。せっけんで洗います。
　b　ビニールぶくろに入れてもらいません。ぬのぶくろを使います。
　c　車にのりません。じてんしゃで行きます。
　d　エレベーターにのりません。かいだんを使います。
　e　ホースで水をながしません。バケツの水で洗います。
2　Make a poster urging people to save water.

今シャワーをしてもいいですか

Misae's host family live on a small farm.

a   Listen to the conversation between Misae and her host mother.

b   Pretend that you are Misae and write an extract in your diary about the incident they describe.

雨がふらない！ 水がない！ かんばつだ！

かんばつの時、ラップが よく うれるそうです。どうしてだと思いますか。水を
せつやくするために、食器に ラップをかぶせて使うんです。後で洗わなくて
も いいですね！ （でもゴミはふえました。ざんねんですね。）

しょっき

分かりましたか

1   Find these expressions in the news item above.

   a   In times of drought …

   b   Use plastic wrapping …

   c   is sold

   d   … covered

   e   … increased

2   Which of the following comments most closely expresses
the meaning of this news item?

   a   We should throw away the dishes to save
washing up.

   b   Trying to save one thing can lead to other
problems.

   c   In times of drought people will do anything.

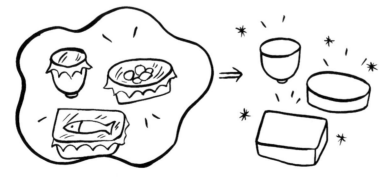

日本の冬は こたつ と おふろで あたたかい

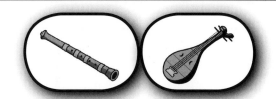

しゃくはち: You are conducting a survey about water usage. Find out about びわ's water usage by reading out each of the statements below. When びわ repeats the whole statement(s) he agrees with, write the letter of his answer in your notebook. Find out how aware びわ is of the value of water by adding up the points.

びわ: Don't look at the page. Listen and repeat the statement you agree with.

Take turns to be the interviewer.

1 はをみがく時...
   a コップ 1 ぱいの水を使います。(3)
   b 水を出して、みがきます。(0)
   c はをみがきません。(1)
2 家の前をそうじする時に...
   a 水でそうじします。(0)
   b ほうきでそうじします。(3)
   c 家の前をそうじしません。(2)
3 車を洗う時に...
   a ホースを使って洗います。(0)
   b バケツに水をためて洗います。(3)
   c 車がないから、洗いません。(3)
4 シャワーをあびる時...
   a 4 分ぐらいあびます。(3)
   b 8 分ぐらいあびます。(2)
   c シャワーが好きだから、20 分から、30 分ぐらいあびます。(0)
5 庭のしばふに水を...
   a 毎日、雨の日も水をまきます。(give water) (0)
   b 一週間 一回、朝はやく、まきます。(2)
   c ひつような時だけ、まきます。(3)
6 じゃ口から水もれしている時に...
   a じゃ口の下にバケツをおいて、後で水を使います。(2)
   b すぐになおします。(fix it) (3)
   c しんぱいしないで、そのまま使います。(1)

Points

16–18   水はとても大切だと思っていますね。
7–15   水は大切だけど、水のせつやくはふべんだと思っていますね。
0–6   水は大切じゃないと思っていますね。

水を大切に使いましょう

かてい (家庭)	household
じゃぐち (じゃ口)	tap
じゅうぶん (十分)	enough, sufficient
すいどう (水道)	water supply
せつやく <する>	saving, to save
ためる ⓡ	to collect, fill
ながす ⓤ	to let out water
はをみがく ⓤ	to brush teeth
ひつよう [な]	necessary, need
へいきん	average
ほうき	broom
ホース	hose
みずもれ (水もれ)	leaking water

雨がふらない！水がない！かんばつだ！

かぶせる ⓡ	to cover (something with)
かんばつ	drought

水の使い方―日本のアイデアー

うえき (うえ木)	pot plant
(お) こめ	uncooked rice
せんたく (洗濯)	washing, laundry
つぎの (次の)	the next
ポンプ	pump

日本の冬はこたつとおふろであたたかい

こたつ	a quilt-covered table with a heater beneath
さいご (の)	the last, final
のこりゆ	left-over warm water
ほんとう (本当)	true, real
わく ⓤ	to heat
おふろがわいた	bath is ready

I can:
- understand ways to save water
- express 'the time when …'
- understand Japanese ways to save water
- express that something is different from …
- express doing things in a different way
- understand Japanese ways of keeping warm in winter
- read and write the following kanji
  切 出 入 洗 庭 次

Appendix

る verbs and う verbs

う verbs are called *godan* verbs in Japanese because the stem has five different inflections which correspond to the five syllable bands on the hiragana chart. る verbs are called *ichidan* verbs because there is only one stem. See pages 185–186 for a summary of all verb forms. The following section explains the う verbs further.

う verbs

The masu form (Band 2)

The syllable before the polite ending *masu* corresponds to the second syllable band on the hiragana chart. Band 2 is called the *masu* band because う verbs always have these syllables before *masu*, *masen*, *mashita*, *masen deshita* and *mashoo*.

Hiragana chart

Band 1	ら	や	ま	ば	な	た	さ	が	か	あ／わ	
Band 2	り		み	び	に	ち	し	ぎ	き	い	These syllables come before *masu*.
Band 3	る	ゆ	む	ぶ	ぬ	つ	す	ぐ	く	う	
Band 4	れ		め	べ	ね	て	せ	げ	け	え	
Band 5	ろ	よ	も	ぼ	の	と	そ	ご	こ	お	

Here is a list of example う verbs in their *masu* form. Read them down the page.

This part does not change →	か	あ		は		お		
	え	よ	そ	した	な	よ	か	か
This syllable changes →	り	み	び	に	ち	し	ぎ	き	い
	ま	ま	ま	ま	ま	ま	ま	ま	ま
Verb ending. This part changes. →	す	す	す	す	す	す	す	す	す
	return	read	play	die	stand	speak	swim	wake	buy

Note:

1 There are no verbs that have ひ before <u>masu</u>.

2 There is only one verb that has に before <u>masu</u> and that is the example given. しにます means die.

3 There are many う verbs that share the same syllable before <u>masu</u>. For example: あるきます、ききます、かきます.

Put the following verbs into groups according to the syllable before *masu*.

1 なおします	4 まちます	7 すわります	10 あらいます	13 ぬぎます
2 ききます	5 いそぎます	8 よびます	11 のります	14 すみます
3 だします	6 のみます	9 もちます	12 あるきます	15 けします

The dictionary form (Band 3)

The syllable that forms the dictionary form ending corresponds to the third syllable band on the hiragana chart. Band 3 is called the dictionary form band because the dictionary form of う verbs always ends with one of these syllables. This form is not only used to list verbs in dictionaries but is also the plain present and future used in informal speech and writing and in grammatical constructions.

Hiragana chart

Band 1	ら	や	ま	ば	な	た	さ	が	か	あ／わ	
Band 2	り		み	び	に	ち	し	ぎ	き	い	
Band 3	る		む	ぶ	ぬ	つ	す	ぐ	く	う	Dictionary form
Band 4	れ		め	べ	ね	て	せ	げ	け	え	
Band 5	ろ		も	ぼ	の	と	そ	ご	こ	お	

Here is the same list of example う verbs in the dictionary form. Read them down the page.

				か		あ		は	お	
え	よ	そ	し	た	な	よ	か	か	
る	む	ぶ	ぬ	つ	す	ぐ	く	う	↓

If you know the *masu* form, making the dictionary form is easy: take off the *masu* and change the い syllable on Band 2 to an う syllable on Band 3.

(れい)

あらいます ⟶ あらい ⟶ あらう
かきます ⟶ かき ⟶ かく

If you know the dictionary form, making the *masu* form is easy: take off the last syllable, change it to the appropriate い syllable and add ます.

(れい)

ふる ⟶ ふり ⟶ ふります
およぐ ⟶ およぎ ⟶ およぎます

Change these verbs to their dictionary form.

| 1 ぬぎます | 3 てつだいます | 5 はきます | 7 つきます | 9 うたいます |
| 2 わらいます | 4 だします | 6 やすみます | 8 わかります | 10 とります |

Note: A few る verbs look like う verbs. You will have to memorise these as they occur. In the vocabulary lists う verbs are indicated ⓤ and る verbs ⓡ.

The nai form (Band 1)

The syllable before *nai* and the forms that come from *nai* (*naide, nakereba, nakutemo, nakutewa*) corresponds to the first syllable band on the hiragana chart. *Nai* is used to make the plain negative in informal speech and writing and in grammatical construction.

Hiragana chart

Band 1	ら	ま	ば	な	た	さ	が	か	あ／わ	plus ない etc
Band 2	り	み	び	に	ち	し	ぎ	き	い	
Band 3	る	む	ぶ	ぬ	つ	す	ぐ	く	う	
Band 4	れ	め	べ	ね	て	せ	げ	け	え	
Band 5	ろ	も	ぼ	の	と	そ	ご	こ	お	

Here is the list of example う verbs in the *nai* form. Read them down the page.

	か		あ			は	お			
え	よ	そ	し	た	な	よ	か	か	
ら	ま	ば	な	た	さ	が	か	わ	
な	な	な	な	な	な	な	な	な	
い	い	い	い	い	い	い	い	い	

Note: Verbs that have a dictionary form of う make the plain negative with わ not あ. So the negative is … わない

The *nai* form of あります is just ない, not あらない.

To change a verb in the *masu* form, remove ます, change the い sound to an あ sound plus ない.

れい

```
          ら
1  すわります + ない ─────────▶ すわらない
          か
2  あるきます + ない ─────────▶ あるかない
```

To change an う verb from the dictionary form to the *nai* form, change the う sound on Band 3 at the end of the verb to the corresponding あ sound on Band 1 and add ない.

れい

```
          ま
1  やすむ + ない ─────────▶ やすまない
          ら
2  かえる + ない ─────────▶ かえらない
```

Change the following verbs to the *nai* form.

1 だす	**3** もつ	**5** ぬぐ	**7** はく	**9** つく	**11** けす	**13** いう	**15** うたう	**17** かう
2 のむ	**4** あそぶ	**6** はいる	**8** ある	**10** とぶ	**12** しぬ	**14** かざる	**16** きく	**18** まつ

The て form

る verbs

Just add て to the stem (the part before *masu*), for example

たべます ——————▶ たべて

みます ——————▶ みて

う verbs

う verbs form five て form groups.

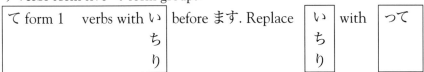

て form 1	verbs with い ち り	before ます. Replace	い ち り	with	って

れい

かいます ——————▶ かって

たちます ——————▶ たって

のります ——————▶ のって

て form 2	verbs with き	before ます. Replace	き	with	いて

れい

かきます ——————▶ かいて

•exception いきます (to go) いって

て form 3	verbs with ぎ	before ます. Replace	ぎ	with	いで

れい

およぎます ——————▶ およいで

て form 4	verbs with し	before ます. Add	て		して

れい

はなします ——————▶ なはして

て form 5	verbs with び に み	before ます. Replace	び に み	with	んで

れい

あそびます ——————▶ あそんで

しにます ——————▶ しんで

よみます ——————▶ よんで

Give the て forms of the following:

1 すわります   5 あるきます   9 やすみます   13 なおします

2 いそぎます   6 うたいます   10 のみます   14 さきます

3 およぎます   7 おくります   11 はきます   15 よびます

4 あらいます   8 かきます   12 もちます   16 かえります

Summary of verb forms

る verbs (ます form)	ない form	Plain present/ future Dictionary form	Meaning
たべ・ます	たべ・ない	たべ・る	to eat
おしえ・ます	おしえ・ない	おしえ・る	to teach
み・ます	み・ない	み・る	to see
い・ます	い・ない	い・る	to be, stay

う verbs (ます form)	ない form	Dictionary form	Meaning
かい・ます	かわ・ない	かう	to buy
かき・ます	かか・ない	かく	to write
だし・ます	ださ・ない	だす	to put out
たち・ます	たた・ない	たつ	to stand
しに・ます	しな・ない	しぬ	to die
とび・ます	とば・ない	とぶ	to fly
よみ・ます	よま・ない	よむ	to read
ふり・ます	ふら・ない	ふる	to fall

Irregular verbs (ます)	ない form	Dictionary form	Meaning
し・ます	しない	する	to do
き・ます	こない	くる	to come

Variations introduced in *Mirai Stage 5*:

たべ・やすい 　　にくい 　　すぎる 　　はじめる	たべ・ない 　　なかった 　　ないで 　　なくてもいい 　　なくてはいけない 　　なければならない 　　なくちゃ 　　なきゃ 　　ないといけない	たべる・じかん 　　とき 　　つもり 　　そう

Summary of verb forms (cont.)

る verbs	て form	た form (plain past)
たべる	たべて	たべた
おしえる	おしえて	おしえた
みる	みて	みた
いる	いて	いた
う verbs	**て form**	**た form**
かう	かって	かった
かく	かいて	かいた
だす	だして	だした
たつ	たって	たった
しぬ	しんで	しんだ
とぶ	とんで	とんだ
よむ	よんで	よんだ
ふる	ふって	ふった
Exception いく	いって	いった
Irregular verbs	**て form**	**た form**
する	して	した
くる	きて	きた

Variations introduced in *Mirai Stage 5*:

たべて・いる ・くださいませんか おしえて・くれない ・あげる つくって・さしあげる ・くれる ・くださる ・もらう ・いただく	たべ・たり

Adjectives

Group 1: い ending adjectives

When the adjective comes before the noun, these adjectives do not change.

（れい）

さむい 日 a cold day　　　　　　おもしろい はなし an interesting story

When the adjective ends the sentence, the adjective changes according to the tense.

（れい）

さむかったです。　　　　　　　It was cold.

おもしろくなかったです。　　　　It was not interesting.

The addition of です makes the statement polite; removing です turns it into plain speech.

Polite form	Plain forms			
	present	past	negative present	negative past
あついです いいです (よい)	あつい いい (よい)	あつかった よかった	あつくない よくない	あつくなかった よくなかった

Note: 1 The old form of いい was よい.

2 The verb endings たい and ない change in the same way as the い adjectives.

Group 2: な ending adjectives

When the adjective comes before the noun な has to be added.

（れい）

べんりな カメラ, a handy camera　　　きれいな ようふく, pretty clothes

When the adjective ends the sentence, the adjective does not change according to the tense.
The word です changes instead.

（れい）

べんりでした。　　　　　　　　It was handy.

きれい｛では ありませんでした。　きれい｛ではなかったです。 It was not clean. (pretty)
　　　｛じゃ ありませんでした。　　　　｛じゃなかった。

To make the plain present and plain past, です itself must change to the plain form.
In the negative, 'ない' changes like an い adjective.

Polite form	Plain forms			
	present	past	negative present	negative past
にがてです	にがてだ	にがてだった	にがて｛ではない 　　　｛じゃない	にがて｛ではなかった 　　　｛じゃなかった

Note: a few な adjectives look like い adjectives because they end with い.
The most common are きれい, ゆうめい, きらい, とくい.

て forms of adjectives	
い adjectives	な adjectives
あつ・くて	べんり・で
よ・くて	きれい・で

Compounds

Unit 1 (page 9)

お姉さん	おねえさん	older sister	高校	こうこう	senior high school	高校生	こうこうせい	high school student
姉妹	しまい	sisters	中学	ちゅうがく	junior high school	十才	じゅっさい	10 years old
有名	ゆうめい	famous	学校	がっこう	school	十六才	じゅうろくさい	16 years old
名前	なまえ	name	小学校	しょうがっこう	primary school	兄弟	きょうだい	brothers, siblings
日本語	にほんご	Japanese	大学	だいがく	university	先生	せんせい	teacher
英語	えいご	English	一年生	いちねんせい	first year student	家族	かぞく	family
言語	げんご	languages	一生	いっしょう	a lifetime	学生	がくせい	student

Unit 2 (page 28)

天気	てんき	weather	元気	げんき	vigour, vitality	一時	いちじ	1 o'clock
二時半	にじはん	half past two	五時間	ごじかん	for five hours	何時	なんじ	what time
手紙	てがみ	letter	(お)手洗い	(お)てあらい	toilet	手足	てあし	hands and feet
上手	じょうず	skilled	下手	へた	unskilful	今年	ことし	this year
今月	こんげつ	this month	今週	こんしゅう	this week	今日	きょう	today
電気	でんき	electricity	電話	でんわ	phone	電車	でんしゃ	train

Names

秋子　あきこ	春子　はるこ	秋山　あきやま	夏目　なつめ	冬川　ふゆかわ	春木　はるき

Unit 3 (page 42)

ご飯	ごはん	food, rice	先生	せんせい	teacher	名前	なまえ	name
夏休み	なつやすみ	summer holiday	冬休み	ふゆやすみ	winter holiday	外国	がいこく	foreign country
昼休み	ひるやすみ	lunchtime	休日	きゅうじつ	holiday	宿題	しゅくだい	homework

Unit 4 (page 60)

赤ちゃん	あかちゃん	baby	赤土	あかつち	red earth	青年	せいねん	young man, youth
青春	せいしゅん	youth	雪水	ゆきみず	slush	花火	はなび	fireworks
花見	はなみ	flower viewing	日曜日	にちようび	Sunday	青空	あおぞら	blue sky
空中	くうちゅう	in the air	空気	くうき	air, atmosphere	空港	くうこう	airport

Unit 5 (page 75)

お正月	おしょうがつ	New Year	買い物	かいもの	shopping	来年	らいねん	next year
来週	らいしゅう	next week	来月	らいげつ	next month	今朝	けさ	this morning
朝ご飯	あさごはん	breakfast	朝食	ちょうしょく	breakfast	早朝	そうちょう	early morning
白人	はくじん	white people	白金	はっきん	white gold	白紙	はくし	blank paper

Unit 6 (page 102)

友達	ともだち	friend	一時間	いちじかん	for one hour	思い出	おもいで	memory
一年間	いちねんかん	for one year	新年	しんねん	New Year	一番	いちばん	the best, most
毎日	まいにち	every day	毎週	まいしゅう	every week	海水	かいすい	sea water
毎年	まいとし	every year	毎朝	まいあさ	every morning	海外	かいがい	overseas

Unit 7 (page 113)

音楽	おんがく	music	午前	ごぜん	a.m.	午後	ごご	p.m.
買い物	かいもの	shopping	食べ物	たべもの	food	強大	きょうだい	powerful
読書	どくしょ	reading	読み物	よみもの	reading material	勉強	べんきょう	study

Unit 8 (page 127, 128)

自分	じぶん	oneself	自転車	じてんしゃ	bicycle	時分	じぶん	time, hour
五分	ごふん	5 minutes	十分	じゅっぷん	10 minutes	新聞	しんぶん	newspaper
生活	せいかつ	life	活気	かっき	liveliness	通学	つうがく	attend school
通行	つうこう	passing	文通	ぶんつう	cor-respondence	交通	こうつう	traffic
住人	じゅうにん	inhabitant	住所	じゅうしょ	residence, address	大事	だいじ	important
仕事	しごと	work	時々	ときどき	sometimes	人々	ひとびと	people
山々	やまやま	mountains	体中	からだじゅう	whole body	体育	たいいく	phys. ed.
私達	わたしたち	we	子供達	こどもたち	children	達人	たつじん	an expert

Unit 9 (page 144)

飲み水	のみみず	drinking water	飲食	いんしょく	eating and drinking	映画	えいが	movie
画家	がか	artist (painter)	同時	どうじ	same time	同名	どうめい	same name
石川	いしかわ	stony river, a surname	石山	いしやま	stony mountain, a surname	有名	ゆうめい	famous
近海	きんかい	adjacent seas	近所	きんじょ	neighbour-hood	近道	ちかみち	shortcut

Unit 10 (page 157)

使い方	つかいかた	how to use	黒板	こくばん	blackboard	白黒	しろくろ	black and white
書道	しょどう	calligraphy	書体	しょたい	style of penmanship	去年	きょねん	last year
水道	すいどう	water supply	柔道	じゅうどう	judo	道具	どうぐ	instrument, tool
広大	こうだい	vast	広々	ひろびろ	extensive	知人	ちじん	acquaintance

Unit 11 (page 167)

水着	みずぎ	swim suit	先着	せんちゃく	first arrival	教会	きょうかい	church
教室	きょうしつ	classroom	音楽室	おんがくしつ	music room	自動	じどう	automatic
自動車	じどうしゃ	car	帰国	きこく	return to one's country	国々	くにぐに	countries

Unit 12 (page 173)

大切	たいせつ	important	切手	きって	stamp	出口	でぐち	exit
出金	しゅっきん	payment	入り口	いりぐち	entrance	入れ物	いれもの	container
入学	にゅうがく	school admission	水洗	すいせん	flushing, washing	洗濯	せんたく	laundry, washing
次々	つぎつぎ	one by one	家庭	かてい	household	石庭	せきてい	rock garden

English–Japanese word list

The following word list contains most of the vocabulary used in the texts. Words have been omitted for which there is no simple English equivalent. This word list is not a dictionary, and students should consult a dictionary for further information about the usage of the words. Verbs are indicated (v). う verbs and る verbs are indicated ⓤ ⓡ.

about	〜について	be told	言われる ⓡ
absolutely	ぜったいに	blunder, mistake	しっぱい
accessories	アクセサリー	boil, heat (v)	わく ⓤ わかす ⓤ
add, include	くわえる ⓡ	borrow	かりる ⓡ
adventure	ぼうけん	both sides	りょうがわ
advise (v)	すすめる ⓡ	bowling	ボーリング
after school	ほうかご	broom	ほうき
afterwards	あとで (後で)	brothers and sisters	きょうだい (兄弟)
aged person	としより	brush, clean (v)	みがく ⓤ
aim at (v)	めざす ⓤ	bubbles	あわ
all right	だいじょうぶ	bucket	バケツ
amusement park	ゆうえんち	burn, be burnt (v)	やける ⓡ
and so	それで	busy	いそがしい
and then	すると	but, nevertheless	けど、けれど
annoying	めいわく	by far	ずっと
anyone	だれか	by the way	ところで
appearance, dress	ふくそう	cabbage	キャベツ
approval	さんせい	calculation	けいさん
approve (v)	さんせい する	call	よぶ ⓤ
art	げいじゅつ	calligraphy	しゅうじ
ascend, go up (v)	あがる ⓤ	carry (v)	はこぶ ⓤ
athletics meetings	うんどうかい	(be) caught	かかる ⓤ
attend school (v)	つうがく する	celebrate (v)	おいわいを する
average	へいきん	change	おつり
awful	ひどい	chat	しゃべる ⓤ
awfully	すごく	China	ちゅうごく (中国)
bad manners	ぎょうぎがわるい	Chinese language	ちゅうごくご (中国語)
bag, sack	ふくろ	choral society	コーラスぶ
baked whole	まるやき	Christmas tree	クリスマス・ツリー
bakery	パンや	Church	きょうかい (教会)
bath	(お) ふろ	City hall	しやくしょ
be caught (v)	かかる ⓤ	classics	クラシック
be born	うまれる (生まれる) ⓡ	cloth	ぬの
beef stock/soup stock	コンソメ	collect, save (v)	ためる ⓡ
be friendly	なかよく する	combine	あわせる ⓡ
be hit, beaten	たたかれる ⓡ	companion	あいて
besides	ほかに	compare (v)	くらべる ⓡ
be put in	いれられる (入れられる) ⓡ	complicated	ふくざつ [な]
besides	ほかに	computer game	ファミコン

come near	ちかづく ⑤		enclose (with a letter) (v)	どうふう する
concern, worry	しんぱい		enjoy (v)	たのしむ (楽しむ) ⑤
congratulations	おめでとう		enjoyment	たのしみ (楽しみ)
construct (v)	たてる ⑥		enough	じゅうぶん (十分)
continue (v)	つづける ⑥		entrance exams	にゅうし
convenience	つごう		entrance hall	げんかん
corner	すみ		envelope	ふうとう
corridor, hallway	ろうか		envious	うらやましい
cosmetics	(お) けしょう		environment	かんきょう
(use) cosmetics	けしょう する		erase	けす ⑤
costume	いしょう		exactly	ちょうど
country	くに (国)		examination, test	しけん
cover (v)	かぶせる ⑥		excuse me	すみません、ごめんなさい
cow	うし		exercise	うんどう
crowd	ひとごみ (人ごみ)		(be) extinguished (v)	きえる ⑥
cruel	ひどい		extraordinary, amazing	えらい
cry (v)	なく ⑤		extravagance, waste	むだづかい
cute, lovely	かわいい		extremely	ずいぶん
dance (v)	おどる ⑤		farm (grazing)	ぼくじょう
danger	きけん [な]		(be) fashionable (v)	はやる ⑤
dark	くらい		feast, delicious food	ごちそう
dawn, morning sun	あさひ (朝日)		feature, report	とくしゅう
decorate (v)	かざる ⑤		feel (v)	かんじる ⑥
decoration	デコレーション		feeling	きもち (気持ち)
decrease (v)	へらす ⑤		feel unwell	きぶん (気分) がわるい
definitely	ぜひ		feminine	おんならしい (女らしい)
demonstration	デモ		festival	まつり
detergent	せんざい		fever	ねつ
diarrhoea	げり		finally	とうとう
die (v) (euphemism)	なくなる ⑤		find (v)	みつける (見つける) ⑥
(be) different (v)	ちがう ⑤		fine, nice	けっこう [な]
direction	ほう		finish (v)	しまう ⑤
disappear (animate)	いなくなる ⑤		fire	かじ (火事)
(inanimate)	なくなる ⑤		fire works	はなび (花火)
dishes, cooking	りょうり		first of all	まず
drain (v)	ながす ⑤		food, meal	しょくじ (食事)
dreadful	ひどい		foreigner	がいこくじん (外国人)
dripping water	みずもれ (水もれ)		for	～よう (用)
driver	うんてんしゅ		for example	たとえば
drop, lower (v)	おとす ⑤		forthcoming	こんど (の)
drought	かんばつ		free time	じゆうじかん (自由時間)
earrings (pierced)	ピアス		freely	じゆうに
earnestly	いっしょうけんめい		funny, amusing	おかしい
economise (v)	せつやく する		furniture	かぐ (家具)
egg	たまご		future (in the)	しょうらい
embarrassed, shy	はずかしい		gentle, kind-hearted	やさしい
empty can	あきかん		germs	バイキン

get on, board (v)	のる ⓤ
gives to me (humble) (v)	くださる ⓤ
go to meet (v)	むかえに行く ⓤ
gradually	だんだん
greatly	だいぶ
graffiti	らくがき
greeting	あいさつ
group, set (counter)	くみ
guidance	あんない
guide (v)	あんない する
gum	ガム
gymnasium	たいいくかん
hang up (v)	ぶらさげる ⓡ
happiness	しあわせ
happy, glad	うれしい
hat	ぼうし
head (counter)	～とう
health(y)	けんこう [な], げんき [な]
heat (v)	わかす ⓤ
here (formal)	こちら
hide (v)	かくす ⓤ
high school	こうこう (高校)
hit (v)	たたく ⓤ
hobby	しゅみ
homework	しゅくだい (宿題)
horse riding	じょうば
hose	ホース
hospital, clinic	びょういん
hot and humid	むしあつい
hot water	(お) ゆ
house (not the speaker's)	おたく
household	かてい (家庭)
housewife	しゅふ
how is? about?	どう (ですか)
hug each other (v)	だきあう ⓤ
hug, cuddle (v)	だく ⓤ
humiliating	くやしい
hurriedly, quickly	いそいで
image	イメージ, えいぞう
important	たいせつ [な]、だいじ [な]
in this way	こういうふうに
increase (v)	ふえる ⓡ
incredible	すごい
inform, let know (v)	しらせる (知らせる) ⓡ
ingredients	ざいりょう
injection	ちゅうしゃ
(be) injured (v)	けがを する

injury	けが
inquire (v)	ちょうさ する
inquiry	ちょうさ
insert, put in (v)	いれる (入れる) ⓡ
instead	かわりに
intently	じっと
interest	きょうみ
interested in (v)	きょうみがある ⓤ
island	しま
it can't be helped	しかたがない
kendoo club	けんどうぶ
kendoo stick	しない
kill (v)	ころす ⓤ
kindly, gentle	やさしい
kiss (v)	キス する
last, final	さいご (の)
(be) late (v)	ちこくを する
(be) lazy (v)	なまけている ⓡ
lazy person	なまけもの
life, living	せいかつ
life (spiritual)	いのち
lively, healthy	げんき (元気) [な]
living room	いま
laugh	わらう ⓤ
long ago	むかし、ずっとまえ (前) に
lonely	さびしい
looks	～そう
luggage	にもつ
magic	まほう
magician	まほうつかい
make (v)	つくる ⓤ
maple trees, leaves	もみじ
manicure	マニキュア
match, game	しあい
mayonnaise	マヨネーズ
meat	(お) にく
meet, see (v)	あう (会う) ⓤ
middle school	ちゅうがっこう (中学校)
mobile phone	けいたいでんわ (けいたい電話)
most, no. 1	いちばん (一番)
move house (v)	ひっこしをする
move (v)	うごく ⓤ
musical instrument	がっき (楽器)
mysterious	ふしぎ [な]
narrow	せまい
nausea	はきけ

necessity	ひつよう	problem	もんだい
need (v)	いる Ⓤ	professional	プロ
neighbourhood	きんじょ	protect (v)	まもる Ⓤ
New Year	(お) しょうがつ (お正月)	pudding	プディング
New Year's Eve	おおみそか	pump	ポンプ
news item, account	きじ	purple	むらさきいろ
next	つぎ (次)	put out, post (v)	だす (出す) Ⓤ
nickname	あだな	question	しつもん
north	きた (北)	rabbit	うさぎ
nothing	なにも + neg	radio-controlled car	ラジコン
number	かず	reading	どくしょ
of course	もちろん	receive (humble) (v)	いただく Ⓤ
old newspaper	しんぶんし (新聞紙)	receive (m)	もらう Ⓤ
on the way	とちゅう	recently	さいきん、このあいだ (間)
one by one	ひとりずつ (一人ずつ)	reception	うけつけ
one's own pace	マイペース	record	きろく
onion	たまねぎ	recycled paper	さいせいし (再生紙)
opinion	いけん	regret, disappointment	ざんねん
oppose (v)	はんたい する	relative, relation	しんせき
opposition	はんたい	remove, take off (v)	ぬぐ Ⓤ
other	ほかの	resemble	にている Ⓡ
outline, gist	あらすじ	reserve, book (v)	よやく する
owner	もちぬし	resurrection	ふっかつ
parents	りょうしん、 おや	rice (uncooked)	(お) こめ
parted, be (v)	わかれる Ⓡ	rich person	かねもち (金持ち)
participate (v)	さんか する	rubbish	ごみ
participation	さんか	rubbish bin	ごみばこ
pass time (v)	すごす Ⓤ	run around (v)	はしりまわる Ⓤ
pass (time), elapse (v)	たつ Ⓤ	runny nose	はなみず
perform (v)	えんそう する	sad	かなしい
performance	えんそう	salt	しお
pick up (v)	ひろう Ⓤ	same	おなじ (同じ)
pig	ぶた	save (v)	ためる Ⓡ
place	ところ	save money (v)	ちょきん する
(be) placed	おいてある Ⓤ	save, rescue	たすける Ⓡ
plan, devise	くふう	saving, economy	せつやく
plan, devise (v)	くふう する	scene	ばめん
plant, sow (v)	うえる Ⓡ	sea water	かいすい (海水)
plastic, vinyl	ビニール	see off (v)	おくりにいく
play (stringed inst.) (v)	ひく Ⓤ		(おくりに行く) Ⓤ
points	てん (点)、てんすう (点数)	self-introduction	じこしょうかい
pop music	ポップス	to introduce self (v)	じこしょうかい する
(be) popular (v)	にんき (人気) がある Ⓤ	sell, be sold (v)	うれる Ⓡ
pot plant	うえき (うえ木)	shape	かたち
prawns	えび	shoe cupboard	げたばこ
prayer	(お) いのり	(be) similar (v)	にている Ⓡ
primary school	しょうがっこう (小学校)	sigh (v)	ためいきをつく Ⓤ

side, next to	よこ	take out, remove (v)	とりだす ⑤
simple	かんたん	take with you (person) (v)	つれていく
skin, peel	かわ		(つれて行く) ⑤
sleepy	ねむい	tap	じゃぐち (蛇口)
slumber, sleep (v)	ねむる ⑤ ねる ⑥	tap water, water supply	すいどう (水道)
smoke (v)	たばこをすう ⑤	tea ceremony club	さどうぶ
snack	おやつ	teacher	きょうし、せんせい (先生)
soap	せっけん	than	～より
socks	くつした	there (formal)	そちら
something	なにか (何か)	therefore	それで
soon	もうすぐ	think (v)	おもう (思う) ⑤
sorry, my apologies	ごめんなさい	this way	こういうふうに
south	みなみ (南)	throw away (v)	すてる ⑥
soy sauce	しょうゆ	ticket	きっぷ、けん、チケット
spacious	ひろい (広い)	ting-a-ling	キンコン カンコン
spare time	ひま	tired, be tired (v)	つかれる ⑥
splendid, de luxe	ごうか [な]	tonight	こんや (今夜)
squid	いか	touch	さわる ⑤
stain, make dirty (v)	よごす ⑤	traditional	でんとうてき [な]
star	ほし	true	ほんとう [の]
state	しゅう (州)	try again (v)	やりなおす ⑤
stay over night (v)	とまる ⑤	tune, condition, form	ちょうし
steadily	しっかり	turkey	しちめんちょう
stick, adhere (v)	つける ⑥	unbearable	たまらない
sticky	ベタベタ	uniform	せいふく
still, after all	やはり、やっぱり	university	だいがく (大学)
stinking	くさい	unpalatable	まずい
stone	いし	usual(ly)	ふつう (に)
stop, quite (v)	やめる ⑥	vegetables	やさい
strict	きびしい	violence	ぼうりょく
strong point	とくい [な]	wash clothes (v)	せんたく する
student who studies abroad	りゅうがくせい (留学生)	washing, laundry	せんたく
success	せいこう	way, manner	～かた (方)
such	そんな	weak	よわい
suit (v)	あう ⑤	weak point	にがて [な]
sunburnt (v)	ひ (日) にやける ⑥	wear on head (v)	かぶる ⑤
supervise (v)	かんとく する	wedding	けっこん
supervision	かんとく	welcome	ようこそ
surprise	びっくり	well now	さて
(be surprised)	びっくり する	what a waste	もったいない
swimming	すいえい	what happened?	どうしたの?
switch on	スイッチ・オン	what shall we do?	どうしたらいい?
table heater	こたつ	which	どちら
tablewear (dishes)	しょっき (食器)	Worcester sauce	ウスターソース
take care	き (気) をつけて、おげん	worry about, care (v)	きにする (気にする)
	きで (お元気で)	wrap up (v)	つつむ ⑤
take care of (v)	(お) せわする		

Japanese-English word list

あ

あいて	companion, other person
あいさつ	greeting
あう ⓤ	to see, to meet, to suit
あがる ⓤ	to come (go) up, to ascend
あきかん	empty can
アクセサリー	accessories
あけまして おめでとう	New Year's greeting
あさひ (朝日)	dawn, sunrise
あだな	nickname
あとで (後で)	afterwards, after
あとに (後に)	afterwards, after
あらすじ	outline, the gist
あらわす ⓤ	show
あわせる ⓡ	combine
あんな (こんな、そんな)	such
あんない <する>	guidance, to guide, to show around

い

いか	squid
いけん	opinion, idea, view
いし (石)	stone
いしょう	costumes
いじわる	bad-tempered, mean
いそがしい	busy
いただく ⓤ	to receive (humble)
いちばん (一番)	the most, number one
いっしょうけんめい	with all my heart, earnestly
いのち	life
いま	living room
いる ⓤ	to need
いれられる (入れられる) ⓡ	be put in
いれる (入れる) ⓡ	to put in, to insert
いわれる (言われる) ⓡ	be told

う

うえき (うえ木)	pot plant
うえる ⓡ	to plant, to sow, to grow
うごく ⓤ	move
うけつけ	reception
ウスターソース	Worcester sauce
うまれる (生まれる) ⓡ	be born
うれしい	happy, glad
うれしくてたまりません	extremely happy
うれる ⓡ	to be sold, to sell
うんてんしゅ	driver
うんどう	exercise, movement
うんどうかい	athletics meeting, sports day

え

えいぞう	image
えび	prawns
えらい	great, amazing, extraordinary
えんそう <する>	performance, to perform

お

おいてある ⓤ	be placed
おいわい <する>	celebration, to celebrate
おおみそか	New Year's Eve
おかしい	funny, amusing
おくりにいく (行く) ⓤ	to go to see off
(お) けしょう <する>	make-up, cosmetics, to make up
(お) げんきで (お元気で)	take care
(お) こめ	uncooked rice
(お) しょうがつ (正月)	New Year
(お) せわ <する>	to take care of
おせわになりました	thank you for taking care of me
(お) ぞうに	soup with *omochi* in it
おたく	your house, someone's house
おつり	change
おとしだま	gift of money at New Year
おどり	dance
おなじ (同じ)	the same
おなじように (同じように)	in the same way
(お) ふろ	bath
おめでとう	congratulations
おもう (思う) ⓤ	to think
(お) もち	bun made of rice flour
おやつ	snack, refreshment
(お) ゆ	hot water
おんならしい (女らしい)	feminine

か

がいこくじん (外国人)	foreigner
かくす ⑤	to hide, to conceal
かざる ⑤	to decorate, to adorn
かぜをひく ⑤	catch cold
かず	number
～かた (方)	way, manner
かたち	shape
がっき (楽器)	musical instrument
かてい (家庭)	household, family
かねもち (金持ち)	rich person
かぶきのけん	tickets for the kabuki
かぶせる ⑤	to cover something with
かぶる ⑤	to wear (on the head)
ガム	gum
かりる ⑤	to borrow
かわ	skin, peel, rind, crust
かわいい	cute, lovely, charming
かわり (に)	substitute, instead
かんきょう	environment, surroundings
かんじる ⑤	to feel
かんたん [な]	simple, easy
かんとく する	supervision, supervisor, to supervise
かんばつ	drought

き

きえる ⑤	to be extinguished, to go out
きけん [な]	danger, risk, dangerous
きこくしじょ (帰国子女)	returnee children
きじ (記事)	news item, report, article
キス する	kiss, to kiss
きた (北)	north
きにする (気にする)	to worry about, care about
きびしい	strict
きぶんがわるい (気分がわるい)	feel unwell
きもち (気持ち)	feeling
キャベツ	cabbage
きょうかい (教会)	church
ぎょうぎがわるい	bad manners
きょうし	teacher
きょうだい (兄弟)	brothers and sisters
きょうみ	interest

きょうみがある ⑤	to have an interest in
きろく	record
きをつけて (気をつけて)	take care, be careful
キンコン カンコン	ting-a-ling
きんじょ	neighbourhood

く

ぐうぐう	zzzz!zzzz!
くさい	stinking
くださる ⑤	to give (to me)
くつした (くつ下)	socks, stockings
くに (国)	country
くふう する	plan, idea, to devise
くみ	a set, a class, counter for sets
クラシック [の]	classical
くらい	dark
くらべる ⑤	to compare
クリスマス・ツリー	Christmas tree
くやしい	humiliating
くれる ⑤	to give (to me)
くわえる ⑤	add, include

け

けいさつ	police
けいさん	calculation, reckoning
げいじゅつ	art
けが <する>	injury, to be injured
げたばこ	shoe cupboard
けっこう [な]	fine, nice
けっこん	wedding, marriage
けす ⑤	erase
けど (informal)	but
げり	diarrhoea
けれど	and, but, nevertheless
げんかん	entrance hall
げんきが (元気) がわく	become high-spirited
げんき (元気) [な]	healthy, energetic, lively
けんこう [な]	health, healthy
けんどうぶ	kendo club

こ

こういうふうに	in this way
ごうか [な]	splendid, de luxe
こうこう (高校)	high school (years 10–12)
こうして	doing it in this way

コーラスぶ	choral society	しょうがっこう (小学校)	primary school
こたつ	heater built under a table	じょうば <する>	horse riding, to ride
ごちそう する	feast, delicious food, to treat	しょうゆ	soy sauce
こちら	here (polite), this way, this	しょうらい	in the future
ごみ	rubbish, garbage, dust	しょくじ (食事) する	food, meal, to eat
ごみばこ	rubbish bin	しょっき (食器)	table ware, dishes
ごめんなさい	I'm sorry, my apologies	しらせる (知らせる) る	to let know, inform
コンソメ	dear stock	しんせき	relative, relation
こんど	forthcoming, next	しんぱい	concern, worry
こんや	this evening, tonight	しんぶんし (新聞紙)	old newspaper

さ

さいきん [の]	recent, lately, latest		
さいご [の]	the last, final		
さいせいし (再生紙)	recycled paper		
ざいりょう	ingredients		
さがす う	look for		
さて	well now		
さどうぶ	tea ceremony club		
さわる う	touch		
さんか する	participation, to participate		

す

すいえい する	swimming, to swim
スイッチ・オン	switch on
すいどう (水道)	water supply, tap water
ずいぶん	extremely
すごい	wonderful, incredible
すごく	awfully, extremely
すごす う	to pass the time
すすめる る	to advise, recommend
(お) すすめ (します)	may I recommend to you (very polite)
ずっと	by far
すてる る	to throw away
すみ	corner
すみません	excuse me, thank you
すると	and then

し

しあい	match, game, bout
しあわせ [な]	happy, fortunate
じきゅう (時給)	hourly pay
しけん	examination, test
じけん	event, incident
じこしょうかい する	self-introduction (to do)
しちめんちょう	turkey
しっかり	steadily, hard, firmly
じっと	fixedly, intently
しっぱい	blunder, failure, mistake
しつもん	question(s)
しない	kendoo fencing stick
しま	island
しやくしょ	city hall
しゃかい (社会)	society
じゃぐち (じゃ口)	tape
しゃべる う	chat, speak
しゅうじ	calligraphy
じゆうじかん (自由時間)	free time
じゅうぶん (十分)	enough, sufficient
しゅくだい (宿題)	homework
しゅふ	housewife
しゅみ	hobby, interest

せ

せいかつ する	life, living, to live
せいこう する	success, to be successful
せいふく	uniform
ぜったい	absolutely
せっけん	soap
せつやく する	saving, to economise
ぜひ	definitely, without fail
せんざい	detergent
せんたく (洗濯) する	laundry, to do washing
せまい	narrow

そ

～そう	looks like
そうしたら	if you do it that way
そちら	there (polite)
それで	and, and so, as a result, therefore

た

たいいくかん	gymnasium
だいがく (大学)	university
だいじ (大事)	important
だいじょうぶ	all right, OK, safe
たいせつ (大切) [な]	important, previous
だいぶ	greatly
だきあう ⓤ	to hug each other
たすける ⓡ	to save, rescue
たたく ⓤ	hit, beat
たたかれる ⓡ	be hit, beaten
だす ⓤ	to put out, post
ただ	merely
たつ ⓤ	pass time
たとえば	for example
たのしみ (楽しみ)	enjoyment
たのしむ (楽しむ) ⓤ	to enjoy
たばこをすう ⓤ	to smoke
たまご	egg
たまねぎ	onion
たまりません / たまらない	unbearable
ため (に)	in order to, for the sake of
ためいきをつく ⓤ	let out a sigh
ためる ⓡ	to save, heap up, fill
だれでも	anyone, everyone
だんだん	gradually

ち

ちがう ⓤ	to be different
ちかづく ⓤ	come near
ちこく <する>	to be late
ちゅうがく (中学)	middle school
ちゅうがっこう (中学校)	middle school
ちゅうごく (中国)	China
ちゅううごくご (中国語)	Chinese language
ちゅうしゃ	injection
ちゅうもん <する>	order, to order
ちょうさ <する>	inquiry, to investigate
ちょうし	form, conditon, tune
ちょうど	exactly, precisely
ちょきん する	to save (money)

つ

つうがく する	attending school, to attend
つかれる ⓡ	to be tired
つぎの (次の)	the next
つく ⓤ	to be turned on, stick to, adhere
つくる ⓤ	to make
つごう	convenience
つづける ⓡ	to continue
つつむ ⓤ	to wrap up
つれて行く ⓤ	to take with you (a person)

て

デコレーション	decoration
てん (点)	points, dot
てんすう	score, points
でんとうてき [な]	traditional

と

どう	how is, how about
どうしたの？	what, what happened?
とうとう	in the end, finally
とくい [な]	strong point, favourite
とくしゅう (特集)	special report, feature
どくしょ する	reading (as a hobby), to do
ところ	place
ところで	by the way
としより	aged person
とちゅう (と中)	on the way
どちら	which
どなる	to yell, shout
とまる ⓤ	to stay (overnight)
とりだす (取り出す) ⓤ	take out, remove

な

ながす ⓤ	to pour out, let run
なかよく <する>	be friendly
なく ⓤ	to cry, weep
なくなる ⓤ	to disappear (inanimate), die (animate)
なにか	something
なにも … neg.	nothing, not anything
なまけている ⓡ	to be lazy
なまけもの	a lazy person

に

にがて [な]	weak point
にく	meat
～に ついて	about
にている ⓡ	resemble, look like

にもつ	luggage, baggage		ひどい	dreadful, awful
ニュー・イヤーズ・イブ	New Year's Eve		ひとごみ (人ごみ)	crowd of people
にゅうし	entrance exams		ひとりずつ (一人ずつ)	one by one
にんきがある (人気がある) ⑤	to be popular, be in vogue		ビニール	plastic, vinyl
			ひま [な]	spare time, leisure

ぬ

ね

の

は

ひ

ふ

へ

ほ

ぬぐ ⑤ — to remove, take off

ねつ — fever
ねむい — sleepy
ねむる ⑤ — to slumber, sleep
ぬの — cloth

のこりゆ — left-over warm water
のる ⑤ — to get on, board

はいきガス — exhaust fumes
バイキン — germs
ばかやろう — fool, idiot
はきけ — nausea
バケツ — bucket, pail, bin
はこぶ ⑤ — to carry, transport
はずかしい — embarrassed, ashamed, shy
はつもうで — New Year visit to shrine
ハナカ — Hanukkah, Jewish festival
はなび (花火) — fireworks
はなみず — runny nose
ばめん — scene
はやる ⑤ — to be in fashion, catch on
はんざい — crime
パンや — bakery
はんこう — rebellion, defame

ピアス — earrings (pierced)
ピアスをする — to pierce the ear, wear earrings
ひく ⑤ — to play (stringed instrument and piano)
ひさしぶり — after a long time
びっくり <する> — to be surprised, amazed
ひっこしをする — to move house
ひつよう — necessity, need

びょういん — hospital, clinic
ひろい (広い) — spacious
ひろう ⑤ — to pick up, gather up

ファミコン — computer games
ふうとう — envelope
ふえる ⓡ — to increase
ふくざつ [な] — complicated
ふくそう — appearance
ふくろ — bag, sack, pouch
ふしぎ [な] — mysterious, miraculous
ぶた — pig
ふつう (に) — usual(ly), generally
ふっかつ — resurrection, revival
プディング — pudding
ぶらさげる ⓡ — to hang up, suspend

へいきん — average, mean
ベタベタ — sticky, tacky
へらす ⑤ — to decrease, reduce

ほう — direction, singling something out
ほうかご — after school
ほうき — broom
ぼうけん — adventure
ぼうし — hat
ほか (に) — besides
ぼくじょう — farm (grazing only)
ほし — stars
ホース — hose
ポップス — pop music
ボーリング — bowling
ほんとう (本当) (に) — true, truly
ほんとうのことを言うと — to tell the truth
ぼうりょく — violence
ポンプ — pump
ほか — other

ま

マイペース	one's own pace
まず	first of all
まずい	unpalatable, unpleasant taste
まつり	festival
マニキュア	manicure, nail polish
まほう	magic
まほうつかい	magician, wizard
まもる ⑤	to protect, guard, defend
マヨネーズ	mayonnaise
まるやき	baked whole

み

みがく ⑤	to brush, clean, polish
みずもれ	leaking water, dripping
みつける(見つける) ⑥	to find
みなみ	south

む

むかえにいく (行く) ⑤	to go to meet, go to welcome
むかし	long ago, in ancient times
むしあつい	hot and humid
むだ	waste
むだづかい	extravagance, waste, squander
むらさき	purple

め

めいわく	annoying
めざす ⑤	to aim at, have an eye on

も

もうすぐ	soon
もちろん	of course, naturally
もちぬし	owner
もったいない	what a waste
もみじ	maple trees, maple leaves
もらう ⑤	to receive
ものがたり	story
もんだい	problem, question, issue

や

やくざ	gangster
やける ⑥	to burn, be burnt
やさい	vegetables
やっぱり	still, I guess, just as I thought
やめる ⑥	to stop, quit, cease
やりなおす ⑤	to do once more, try again

ゆ

ゆうえんち	amusement park

よ

ようこそ	welcome
よかったら	if it is all right (good)
よこ	side, next to
よごす ⑤	to stain, make dirty
よやく する	booking, to book, reserve
～より	than ～
よぶ ⑤	call
よわい	weak
～よう (用)	for ～

ら

らくがき	graffiti

り

りゅうがくせい	student who studies abroad
りょうがわ	both sides
りょこう	journey
りょうしん	parents
りょうり	dishes, cooking

ろ

ろうか	corridor, hallway

わ

わかす ⑤	to boil (water), heat
わかれる ⑥	be parted
わく ⑤	to heat
わらう ⑤	laugh

Index of grammatical points

Acknowledgements

Special thanks are due to the following people who made valuable contributions to all the Mirai 5 materials.

Calligraphy: courtesy of Katsuaki Takizawa, Reiko Kashiwagi and Miwa Moriwaki

Voices: Shingo Usami, Chika Akutsu, Takahiro Ono, Tomonori Takei, Tomoko Koganezawa, Moe Masano and Yoko Masano.

Audio engineer: Steve Francis.

Music and sounds: Greg Parke.

Other assistance: Yutaka Kakimoto, Shingo Usami and Miwa Moriwaki.